**LIFE SKILL**

# THIS IS WHAT YOU'RE MISSING

## It's Time To Get It Back

## ERIK HILL

# Table of Contents

# Chapter 1:

# 7 Crucial Life Skills To Have

Life skills is a term used to describe many of your abilities to deal effectively with everyday problems. Whether it's problem-solving, learning decision-making, or acquiring communication skills, life skills expand your thinking and can be helpful in both your personal and professional endeavors.

Here are some essential life skills that everyone should learn and master, regardless of age, gender, location, or situation.

## 1. Creativity

Creativity is considered one of the essential life skills you can possess. Creativity helps you better solve problems and allows you to see things from a different perspective. Thinking creatively in your personal life or at work can help you think outside the box, come up with fresh ideas and strategies, and better deal with uncertainty.

Other benefits of creativity include:

1. You can express yourself candidly and honestly.
2. Reduce stress and anxiety.
3. Give a sense of purpose.
4. Improving thinking and problem-solving skills.
5. It makes you feel proud and accomplished.

## 2. Problem-Solving

Another helpful life skill to learn and master is problem-solving. Addressing issues that matter to organizations and individuals puts you in control of your environment. Identifying and fixing the root cause of the problem can bring you great satisfaction and success. As you face and overcome many obstacles in your lifetime, troubleshooting can help you:

1. Tests your ability to analyze information and evaluate situations.
2. Propose new strategies to solve problems.
3. Increase your self-esteem and ability level.

## 3. Communication

Effective communication is a life skill that will take you far, both personally and professionally. You'll meet people from all walks of life throughout your life, so knowing how to be actively involved can help strengthen relationships, increase productivity, and build trust. Other benefits of communication skills include:

1. Improving Relationships at Work.
2. It helps you stay organized.
3. Boost self-esteem.
4. It enables you to create a successful family.
5. Providing opportunities to participate in community life.

# 4. Leadership

Understanding the power and value of leadership is an essential lifelong learning skill that can profoundly impact the lives of others. Leaders not only have control, they know how to motivate, inspire, and empower others. To be a successful leader, you need to teach them to see the strengths of others and to believe in their worth. Leadership can benefit all areas of your life by helping you:

1. Strengthening communication skills.
2. Character development.
3. Build trust.

Leadership skills can be acquired through experience and education.

## 5. Critical Thinking

Learning to think critically is critical to future success. Responsible, productive, and independent thinking can help in all areas of life. Thinking systematically helps improve the way you express your thoughts and ideas.

Some of the essential benefits of critical thinking are:

1.  It helps you make better decisions.
2.  Make you happier.
3.  Better relationship.

Make sure your comments are educated and well informed. Critical thinking also transcends cultural norms and is open to those around you, helping you learn and understand other factors that can influence the decisions of others.

## 6. Self-Awareness

Self-awareness refers to recognizing or recognizing emotions, beliefs, behaviours, and motivations, among other traits, including strengths and weaknesses. Self-awareness is an essential life skill because it allows us to understand better who we are, how we feel, and what makes us unique and different from others. By becoming self-aware, you can make lifestyle changes that will help you think more positively. Here are some key benefits of self-awareness:

1.  Increased communication.
2.  Rich emotional intelligence.
3.  Improve your listening and empathy skills.
4.  Improving Leadership and Opportunities.

# 7. Empathy

In addition to being assertive, it is imperative to empathize with the people around you. Understanding the feelings of others and showing compassion and support can help us respond appropriately. Whether hanging out with a loved one or showing interest in someone at work, empathy can build trust and eliminate conflicts with others.

Along with interpersonal and challenging skills, life skills are essential, and we cannot deny it. The impact of learning skills on your life is enormous. There are several life skills. In this article, I have mentioned some essential life skills that must be learned.

# Chapter 2:

# 7 Ways To Get Clear On What You Want To Achieve In Life

Over time, you might be wondering what makes a person successful and why some people achieve success easier than others? The answer may differ from person to person, but it is a lot more than just setting a goal. As we become clear on our definition of success, it usually changes our perspective on life. With different insights such as these, our goal becomes more directive, and our achievement and motivation levels increase.

Here are 7 Ways to Get Clarity:

## 1. Success and Mindset Go Hand in Hand

The first and foremost tip of becoming successful is to know what success means for you. When you identify this, you will be directed towards your objective or goal, making it easier to achieve it. The second part is your mindset, as it plays a massive role in your success. You might notice that although you might be doing the same thing as hundreds of others, you still aren't getting anywhere. Therefore, you should develop a success mindset instead of being frustrated with it. Below are some ways to help you get clear on what you want to achieve in your life and develop a success mindset.

## 2.  Be Clear on Your Version of Success

Gaining clarity will positively affect your mindset, and it's vital to being and feeling successful. We might know what success means to us in our unconscious mind, but we aren't precisely implementing it in our everyday life. This can make it challenging to access our truth. The need to communicate with ourselves honestly and find some answers arises in such situations. We need to sit somewhere quiet, meditate, and ask ourselves about what we want in life. The answers might not come straight away, but it is essential to know your version of success and what you associate with it.

## 3.  Stretch Yourself

When setting our goals, it's crucial to step out of our comfort zone and include a few elements that will help us stretch and grow to achieve those goals. These might be doing something that you are usually not comfortable with or afraid of doing, such as public speaking, or simply learning a new skill that doesn't come easy on you. By doing this, you will help set a breakthrough goal that would represent a quantum leap.

Examples of breakthrough goals include publishing a book, starting a business, or quitting your current job to get a new one. Of course, material goals are essential, but it all comes down to becoming a life master. The most significant benefit we receive while pursuing our dreams is who we become in the process. As motivational philosopher Jim Rohn advises, "You should set a goal big enough that in the process of achieving it, you become someone worth becoming."

## 4. Work on Your Goals Daily

Please make a list of all your goals and go through them every day to make sure your subconscious mind is focused on what you want. No matter how slow or small, your progress is, it counts as long as you decide not to give up and keep going. As the old joke runs, "How do you eat an elephant? One bite at a time." Similarly, steady progress in bite-sized chunks will eventually put the huge goals into reach. Thus, success isn't a one-time thing, but rather it is a system of gradual efforts.

## 5. Your Goals Should Impact Others

There's not a single person on this earth who can say that he got successful on his own, without any help from anyone. The truth is, we always need a helping hand in the process of becoming something. As soon as we commit to big dreams and goals and go after them, our subconscious mind comes up with big creative ideas to make all of them happen. Then, we will start attracting the people, opportunities, and resources that we need to make our dreams come true. Big dreams not only inspire us but also compel others to play a bit too. When you discover that accomplishing something just isn't for you but also contributing to the betterment of others, it will accelerate the accomplishment of the goal.

## 6.   Reflect and readjust without beating yourself up:

Reflection is one of the most critical success tips, yet it is one of the most crucial elements often ignored or forgotten to rush to the finishing line. For each action that we take, we must be aware of whether it worked or not and then be prepared to change what we are doing until we achieve the outcome. Reflection helps us with all of this. It's ineffective if we just run full steam ahead blindly without pausing for a progress check. It is also important to be kind with yourself when reflecting, as beating yourself up will do no good to you. On the contrary, it will lower your self-esteem and makes it difficult for you to work up to your full potential.

## 7. Take good care of your mind and body:

Our mind and body play a vital role in how successful we become. Therefore, it is crucial to adopt the physiology and psychology of excellence. We must understand that our mind can impact our physical health and our body, too, has an enormous effect on our emotional state. If we feel low in energy and have negative thoughts, it can immensely affect how we perform our daily activities. Nurture your mind, body, and soul, your performance will excel, and you will experience more successful outcomes.

## Conclusion

Take a set of rules on what and how you want to achieve things in your life. Implement them daily and consistently, and you will begin to know what's important to you, which will give you a solid foundation to develop a clear mindset and achieve your goals

# Chapter 3:

# Focus and Concentrate

We all need to become a little distracted every now and then. I get it; it is essential to do these things to keep our brains engaged and active. But we are not the machine that we think we are. We try to reach our goals, and some of us get very close to doing so. But rarely do we get to end the tasks with perfection by doing them the way it was meant to be done.

A very small proportion of people within us get things done not long after they take them on. And these people get them done better than anyone else. But why only so little can do it?

Let me ask you a question; what do you want out of life? What do you want out of education, out of a job, out of relationships? What is it that you are searching for? What do you want to achieve when you take a task? I am sure everyone would have different reasons and motives for all these questions. But here is what I think; You are looking for perfection. But you are not dedicated enough towards those things to achieve that.

You see, there are people who are devoted to a level of obsession. These people work so hard that they start to neglect everything else except their work. Although this is not the way to go around life, you still can't call these people stupid. Because more than often, these are the people on the top of the food chain. These people are on top of everything they touch or do. Why? Because they are focused enough and smart enough to concentrate on what they think is most important to them.

These people have a habit of taking on the things that matter the most to them, which they think can help them gain the ultimate success. They know when to give in to their desires for distraction, and for them, that time is never. So, they keep fighting against all odds giving up all desires of leisure and pleasure. These people have a different reality than the rest of the world, and they make the world realize that what was good was their own dreams.

These people dream of doing and doing as they dream. They work and grind till the time they make every little detail of their dream into the vivid reality that everyone else dreams of their whole life. These people don't care about the results, only about the task itself. Because they know that if they stick to a job long enough, they are meant to become good at it.

If you want to be remembered, remember to keep your priorities straight and your vision focused. Choose the distractions that take you closer to your achievements. Don't even think about the things that make you relax and lose focus. You will be satisfied for that small while, but that moment you lost could never be paid with any hard work ever again.

# Chapter 4:

# Commit To A Specific Goal

A lot of us talk about what we are going to do. A lot of us have a lot on our to-do list that we are going to pursue or that we want to achieve. We all have ambitions, plans, goals, and dreams that we walk around telling everyone. But how many of us are actually doing something to achieve these goals?

The question we ask ourselves is that what are the things that we aspire to? What are the things that we want at no cost? What are the things that will bring us the ultimate happiness?

But none of us ask this; "What is the most important thing that I want to do today?".

The reality of this modern era is that we are busy with so many things that we don't have a clear image of anything anymore. Everything around us is going on and on and we are a slave to everything. Because we think that everything is equally important!

We want to have everything that the media showcases. We want all the glamour and all the success and every petty little thing. But none of us are actually getting any of that!

We need to have a discussion with ourselves once and for all; what is it that we are interested in, and what is it that we are committed to?

Let me clarify this a bit. You have a lot of things that you must do every day for a sustainable life cycle, but out of this daily grunt, what is that you are interested or curious to have, and what is it that must have at any cost?

I am sure you won't be able to come up with much! Because in life, not every stone is worth turning over. Not every tunnel is meant to be searched. Not every seed needs to be sown.

It's not bad to be curious about everything! Curiosity is what makes you set goals. But the reality is that you have one life and a small energy threshold. So why use it to gather everything? Why not put it all in just one basket at a time and let everything become somehow related to that?

If you are committed to a lot of things, you will try to master everything that doesn't even pair with any other thing. You will be distracted every hour of every day. Because you have put your eggs in so many baskets that you have lost count of the baskets.

But if you have one simple, yet important goal or dream, you will have a lot of time mastering a set of skills that complement each other at every step. This will not only increase your chances of getting to that goal but will also help minimize the time you need to reach that goal.

The less time it takes to achieve one, the more life you have ahead to plan and struggle for countless more goals.

# Chapter 5:

# 5 Habits For An Extremely Productive Day

Our productivity and efficiency during the day are variables of several factors. Some days seem better, the sun a little brighter than normal, the food tastes sweeter and the mood lighter. In such days, unmatched joy bubbles within us increasing our productivity exponentially. Many people cannot choose when to experience these days. Instead, they are at the mercy of their emotions and the influence of other people who can ruin their day whenever they please.

Here are five habits for an extremely productive day:

## 1. Plan For Your Day Beforehand.

Failure to plan is planning to fail. A plan is an integral part of success. It means that you understand the obligation you have to live the day ahead and the duties and responsibilities in your in-tray. A plan will help you check all the boxes on your to-do list, and you can track your progress in each.

In planning for your day, you will know the resources that you have and those that you lack. It is also possible to budget on your means earlier rather than waiting for the actual day and start scampering for resources. A wise man does not live on a borrowed budget but within his own.

A good plan is a job half done. Your day will be more productive when nothing takes you by surprise because you would have anticipated every occurrence beforehand, and it will find you armed with a solution.

## 2. Wake Up Early

The early bird catches the worm. Punctuality is very important if you want to have a productive day. An early riser has a fresh and clear mind compared to those who wake up late and start their routine fast because they are behind schedule. They do not have the advantage of calmness and composure because they want to make up for time lost. This exposes them to error and ridicule from their enemies if they fail, which is imminent because of their inaccuracy.

When one wakes up early, one has an advantage over other people. They can open their businesses or start their work earlier than their competitors do. They maximize their productivity because they have created enough time for each task they had scheduled. Consider waking up early to have an extremely productive day.

## 3. Do Not Bite More Than You Can Chew

This calls for sobriety in the handling of tasks and designing of goals. The pressure to outdo yourself can be overwhelming enough to make you lose focus on what is at stake. It is paramount to set realistic and achievable goals so that you can concentrate on them. Shun anything that presents itself to you that is beyond your ability no matter how attractive it seems.

The power of self-control is at play. Resist the temptation of going out of your way to prove a point for the sake of it. Instead, fully concentrate on what you had planned. Schedule anything outside your plan to the following day. It is far from procrastination because in this case, you have a clearly defined timeline on when to actualize your plans.

Failure to develop this habit will lead you to a situation where you have many unfinished tasks. This is not productivity, by all standards. Focus on what you can manage and do it efficiently.

## 4. Avoid Negative Company

A negative company will derail your progress and work. When you associate yourself with such people, you will not see the unseen benefit in challenges and instead, you will focus on the undone, incomplete, and failed bits of your work. Failure is contagious. If you constantly surround yourself with a clique of failures, you too shall fail.

To have a productive day, have friends who share your vision. You will blossom under their shade, and they will encourage you in your work. This will show you possibility even when you see failure and doom. In their company, your days will be productive and joyful.

## 5. Look At The Bigger Picture

As you seek to have productive days, look at the bigger picture. It will make you focus on the greater plan you have rather than petty squabbles and meaningless distractions that come your way. The bigger picture will always remind you of your cause and inspire you to live up to it even when challenges come your way.

When you pay attention to the above five habits, you will have extremely productive days. It all lies in your effort to adopt them.

# Chapter 6:

# 5 Tips for A More Creative Brain

Nearly all great ideas follow a similar creative process, and this article explains how this process works. Understanding this is important because creative thinking is one of the most useful skills you can possess. Nearly every problem you face in work and life can benefit from creative solutions, lateral thinking, and innovative ideas.

Anyone can learn to be creative by using these five steps. That's not to say being creative is easy. Uncovering your creative genius <u>requires</u> <u>courage</u> and <u>tons of practice</u>. However, this five-step approach should help demystify the creative process and illuminate the path to more innovative thinking.

To explain how this process works, let me tell you a short story.

## A Problem in Need of a Creative Solution

In the 1870s, newspapers, and printers faced a very specific and very costly problem. Photography was a new and exciting medium at the time. Readers wanted to see more pictures, but nobody could figure out how to print images quickly and cheaply.

For example, if a newspaper wanted to print an image in the 1870s, they had to commission an engraver to etch a copy of the photograph onto a steel plate by hand. These plates were used to press the image onto the page, but they often broke after a few uses. This process of photoengraving, you can imagine, was remarkably time-consuming and expensive.

The man who invented a solution to this problem was named Frederic Eugene Ives. He became a trailblazer in the field of photography and held over 70 patents by the end of his career. His story of creativity and innovation, which I will share now, is a useful case study for understanding the five key steps of the creative process.

## A Flash of Insight

Ives got his start as a printer's apprentice in Ithaca, New York. After two years of learning the ins and outs of the printing process, he began managing the photographic laboratory at nearby Cornell University. He spent the rest of the decade experimenting with new photography techniques and learning about cameras, printers, and optics.

In 1881, Ives had a flash of insight regarding a better printing technique.

"While operating my photo stereotypes process in Ithaca, I studied the problem of the halftone process," Ives said. "I went to bed one night in a state of brain fog over the problem, and the instant I woke in the morning saw before me, apparently projected on the ceiling, the completely worked out process and equipment in operation."

Ives quickly translated his vision into reality and patented his printing approach in 1881. He spent the remainder of the decade improving upon it. By 1885, he had developed a simplified process that delivered even better results. As it came to be known, the Ives Process reduced the cost of printing images by 15x and remained the standard printing technique for the next 80 years.

Alright, now let's discuss what lessons we can learn from Ives about the creative process.

## The 5 Stages of the Creative Process

In 1940, an advertising executive named James Webb Young published a short guide titled, A Technique for Producing Ideas. In this guide, he made a simple but profound statement about generating creative ideas.

According to Young, innovative ideas happen when you develop new combinations of old elements. In other words, creative thinking is not about generating something new from a blank slate but rather about taking what is already present and combining those bits and pieces in a way that has not been done previously.

Most importantly, generating new combinations hinges upon your ability to see the relationships between concepts. If you can form a new link between two old ideas, you have done something creative.

Young believed this process of creative connection always occurred in five steps.

1. **Gather New Material.** At first, you learn. During this stage, you focus on 1) learning specific material directly related to your task and 2) learning general material by becoming fascinated with a wide range of concepts.

2. **Thoroughly Work Over the Materials in Your Mind.** During this stage, you examine what you have learned by looking at the facts from different angles and experimenting with fitting various ideas together.

3. **Step Away From the Problem.** Next, you put the problem completely out of your mind and do something else that excites you and energizes you.

4. **Let Your Idea Return To You.** At some point, but only after you stop thinking about it will your idea come back to you with a flash of insight and renewed energy.

5. **Shape and Develop Your Idea Based On Feedback.** For any idea to succeed, you must release it out into the world, submit it to criticism, and adapt it as needed.

# Chapter 7:

# 5 Tips to Doing Unique and Meaningful Work

When you think about meaningful work, you think about Mother Theresa or Princess Diana or maybe Peace Corp workers or school teachers and nurses. All of these are great and meaningful jobs. But not everyone can raise money and attention to help get landmines cleared, nor can (or should) everyone try to teach second grade. And if blood makes you faint, nursing isn't a great idea for you either.

So, how can you make your job meaningful work, even when it's not directly making anyone's life better? These five suggestions will change your job from tedious work to meaningful work.

## 1. Look at the Big Picture

Why does your job exist? You <u>could be an HR manager</u>, a grocery store cashier, or a tech company CEO. Each of these jobs is necessary to make the world a better place.

Because this is no longer an agrarian society, you need the grocery store cashier to get food. CEOs of well-managed companies provide goods and services to the community <u>and jobs with paychecks for many people</u>. And HR managers can make people's lives much better by <u>helping them</u>

progress in their careers, finding and providing the best benefits, and hiring great people.

If you just look at the tasks in front of you, you'll forget how you contribute to the community as a whole.

## 2.  Treat Each Other With Kindness

A kind person can change everyone's day from drudgery to fun. Yes, work is still working, and sometimes it's hard, but working with the right people can make you look forward to working even if the job is hard work.

One man who worked for a brewery as a delivery man could have seen his job as hard work and struggle. After all, his job duty was to drive from restaurant to restaurant, carrying huge kegs of beer and taking out the old, empty ones. But, the people in many restaurants cheered when the beer guy came in with the beer kegs. Their act of kindness changed his job from drudgery to one that he loved.

## 3.  Work Hard

How does working hard make a job meaningful? Well, hard work often equals success. When you succeed in your job, you help others in your department succeed in their jobs. When your whole department succeeds, the company succeeds. That is pretty meaningful.

Additionally, hard work is easier than avoiding work. Think about it: when you have to worry if your boss knows how much time you're spending surfing the internet, that adds another layer of complexity to your job. When you're working hard all of the time, and your boss drops by, it's not a big deal.

When you keep on top of your work, you have lowered stress levels. Now, of course, some people are overburdened and cannot accomplish everything. You might start feeling like, "I can't get everything done, so why bother?" These feelings of stress and failure can pose a huge temptation, but don't give in. First of all, you'll start to feel like your job just isn't meaningful—it's just work. Second, that adds additional stress on top of your head.

What you do instead is go to your boss and say directly, "I have five tasks on my plate right now. I can do four effectively, or I can do a lousy job on all five. Which would you prefer?" or "I have five tasks on my plate right now. I only have time to get three of them done. Which two should I skip?"

## 4. Look Outside of Your Job

Does your meaningful work have to be your day job? Of course not. Sometimes your day job can fund your meaningful work. Work-life balance means having a life. Whether it's through your family, church, charity, art, or whatever is important to you, you need a paycheck to support that.

You don't have to fulfill all of your needs through your paid job. You don't even need to feel guilty that you're working for a large corporation rather than a small non-profit. It's not bad to earn money. You find your meaning in how you can spend that money.

## 5.  Consider Changing Jobs

If you just can't see how your current job is meaningful, and you can't figure out a way to make your job meaningful work, then perhaps it's time for you to move on. If your job doesn't bring you joy, doesn't allow you to support your family or essential charitable causes, and doesn't help the community, then maybe it's not the right job for you.

No one has a skill set that is so tiny and unique that there is only one job in the world that would suit them. And if you have no marketable skills, get training in new skills. You don't have to invest in a college degree if that's not your goal.

# Chapter 8:

# 6 Habits To Impress Your Boss and Thrive

It is still unclear to a majority of people what their bosses and employers want from them. Some expressly make it crystal to their employees their expectations of them while others are reserved. What is clear though, is that bosses worldwide have a common goal – to make a profit. It is the major reason why they hired people in their companies to work for them.

Many employees wrongly believe that unless their superiors make a complaint against them, then their work is satisfactory. This notion is a fallacy. Satisfactorily is not the threshold of competency but uniqueness and creativity.

Here are six common habits to impress your boss and thrive:

## 1. Be Unique and Creative

The question employees fail to answer honestly is what they bring to the table. What is it that makes you stand out in the company you work for? It is not your education level because there are many qualified learned people with your skills. Neither is it the duration you work in the company because you receive remuneration for it.

You should be creative in your work and add value to the company. Your devotion to your work will impress your boss because it is uncommon. Ideally, you ought to be irreplaceable in your workplace for you to gain favor and earn a promotion.

## 2. Ensure Proper Communication

Communication is the master key to unlocking conflicts and misunderstandings at the workplace. It is important to ensure proper communication with your boss in your working relationship. You will be able to explain yourself and raise any pertinent issue that affects your work if you have good communication with them.

When you communicate effectively, your superiors will understand you better than if you have poor communication skills or none at all. It may come out as rudeness or ignorance when you communicate ineffectively with your boss. To thrive and gain favor with him/her, build on your communication.

### 3. Never Outshine Your Master

In his famous book, *48 laws of power*, Robert Greene writes this as his first law. It is prudent never to outshine your master and instead let him appear smarter than you are even if it may not be the case. This speaks life to the respect of hierarchy between your boss and yourself. Never make him appear dumb or lame duck by attracting glory to yourself.

Honor your boss both in your speech and in your actions. This will make you find favor in their eyes and you will thrive in your workplace. It does not imply that you should not give any smart suggestions to your bosses but you should do it in a manner that does not usurp their authority.

### 4. Have Integrity

Integrity is the quality of honesty and transparency that one may have. You are misplaced and out of order if your boss cannot trust you to do a task without supervision. Worse is that you are in a bad light if you fall short of honesty and cannot be trusted with the management of resources.

Leaders and bosses are universally interested in people of integrity who will fairly work for them. They want people they will trust to oversee the rest and take their organizations to the next level. The lack of integrity is the biggest turn-off for bosses no matter how qualified employees could be. Uphold integrity to impress your boss and you shall thrive.

## 5. Share Their Vision For The Company

The hiring of managers is tedious and sometimes the competent candidates could not be having the passion of the business at heart. Their remunerations could be their greatest motivation. Routine checks and job evaluations could reveal such hidden traits in employees.

Nevertheless, you need to share the vision of the company with your employer for them to trust you with their resources. People who share the company vision impress hiring managers and owners because their salary is not the sole motivation to work.

## 6. Be Punctual

It is prudent to be punctual in your job. Punctuality is the act of being on time, never late for anything. You should report to work on time, complete assigned tasks on time, and even submit reports required from you on time. Being punctual is a sign of dedication to your job. This act alone will make your boss have a soft spot for you.

In conclusion, when you develop these six habits, you will impress your boss and thrive at your workplace.

# Chapter 9:

# 6 Routine Building Strategies

Creating a positive everyday life is an investment in yourself and a way to do your best for the rest of the world. It also offers additional benefits such as structuring, building the habit of moving forward, and creating the momentum to keep going when you feel powerless to act. Following a daily routine can help you set priorities, limit procrastination, track goals, and be healthier. As Tynan, author of Superhuman by Habit, puts it, this reduces your reliance on your will and motives because a habit is "an action you take consistently with little or no effort or thought".

Feel free to try a new habit and see how it works for you. If they give you energy and inspiration, keep going... If not, keep trying new things until you find one that works. The key is to help you maximize yourself on every level possible by creating regular, consistent daily patterns that will take you where you want to go in life. Now let's move on to a few things you can do in your everyday life to achieve higher mental levels (i.e. more extraordinary brain power and clarity!).

# 1. Get Positive: Start the Day with A Mantra

According to the Mayo Clinic, thinking positively can help you manage stress and improve health. "Today will be the best day!"

Every day, as soon as you get out of bed, you should start saying these simple sentences (out loud). And yes, say to yourself in the morning after a night so short, or when you wake up with the weight of the world on your shoulders. Why? These six words lifted the mood for days to come. It's not the events that make your day good or bad, and it's your reaction to them. As Jim Rohn said, "You rule the day, or the day rules you."

You want to put your heart into good condition immediately. Because if you don't, you will try to tell yourself the wrong thing... But with positive thinking, you can overcome it. Ben Franklin asked himself every morning: What good can I do today?

Choose a phrase or question that resonates with you. It can be as simple as saying "thank you" out loud with a smile and acknowledging that you have a gift the next day.

# 2.   Be Proactive: Don't Check Your Email First

Do you check your email or social media accounts as soon as you wake up in the morning? Then start your day reactively rather than proactive. As Jocelyn K. Gley writes in her book Manage Your DaytoDay, "The problem with this approach is that it means spending most of your day on someone else's priorities."

For example, if you receive an email requesting work-related documents, you may need to provide them immediately, even if you plan to do sideline marketing. Or you open Facebook and see one of your friends is in crisis, and that can become your focus and prevent you from focusing on your problem or concern. Start your day by focusing on yourself. Then you will be in a much better position to help others and achieve more throughout the day.

## 3. Mentally Prepare: Visualize Your Success

Some of the best athletes in the world use visualization to prepare themselves to excel in their sports mentally. Close your eyes and imagine that you are the best and the best. Visualize your best results to place yourself in a shining situation. Include as much detail as possible in your visualizations by using all your senses and making your "training" more powerful.

## 4. Read a Book (Even If It's Just a Page)

Reading books has many scientific benefits. According to Emory University research, reading increases your intelligence, boosts your mental abilities (for up to five days), and may even enhance your capacity to empathize with others. Reading has also been shown to be more than half the risk of getting Alzheimer's... All of this helps to put your mind at ease simultaneously!

## 5. Make Yourself Accountable: Enlist a Partner or Mentor

Make a list of three people you trust and admire. Talk to each of these people and discuss exactly what you want to achieve. After the conversation, decide who will be responsible for the specific milestone you want to achieve.

## 6. Reward Yourself

If you consistently fall into the routine, reward yourself with something fun. For example, if your goal is to learn how to clean up a mess every night before bed, reward yourself with new slippers to enjoy in a clean home.

A healthy routine allows you to maintain the highest possible level of work in the three dimensions of existence: mind, body and spirit. It would help if you had it to get better. It would be best if you had this to keep looking at opportunities and seeing problems as "situations". In short, I need you so that you can be free.

# Chapter 10:

# 6 Ways To Attract Your Potential

Do you sometimes feel like you're wasting your potential? And do you also feel unsure about how you can even reach your full potential? If so, you're like any other ambitious person who wants to make the best of his/her life. Because to me, that's what "reaching your potential" means.

We all have limited time on our hands. Some live longer than others. But you and I both know that it's not about how *long* you live, it's about *what you do* with the time you're alive. It's about leaving everything on the table and making sure you live up to your inner drive. Look, when I talk about reaching your potential, I'm not talking about what other people or society thinks we should do with our lives.

When you chase empty goals and objects, you become restless. Instead, chase your *own* potential and forget about everything external. Become the best person you can be. That's the only honourable aim there is. We identified 6 skills that will help you achieve your full potential. Here they are.

## 1. Self-Awareness

You must be comfortable with who you are and what you are. Don't try to be something you're not. And don't try to change yourself just because others tell you to. Instead, know who you are. And if you don't know, find out. Read, write, think, talk. That's self-awareness: It only requires you to be aware of your thoughts. And when you're self-aware, you automatically learn more about who you are—which is called self-knowledge. But it all starts with being aware. No awareness? No knowledge.

## 2. Leadership

First, focus on yourself. Fix your own problems. Become a stable person who you can rely on. When you do that, focus on inspiring others to do the same. The best way to help others is to teach them to rely on themselves. Sick and narcissistic people want to make people dependent on them. Leaders teach others to be independent. How? By setting a good example. There's no better way to lead.

## 3. Writing

Better writing leads to better thinking. And better thinking leads to better communication. Better communication leads to better results in your career. "What?! I never thought the writing was that important!" When you get good at one thing, it will help you to get better at other things.

You see? It was only when I started writing that everything "clicked." <u>When you become a better writer, you can easily express yourself and start making connections.</u> That will improve your career in ways you never imagine.

## 4. Mindfulness

My definition of mindfulness might be different than yours. To be clear, I'm not talking about meditation, yoga, or Zen Buddhism. I'm talking about being a calm and mindful person. A person who's in control of their thoughts and emotions. A person who's solid as a rock. A person who others can rely on. But achieving that inner peace requires much training. I don't think we can ever fully master this skill. But by practicing control over our thoughts, we can get better. My favourite way to become more mindful is to be present. The more I *stay* in the present moment, the more mindful I am. The aim is never to be lost in thoughts. It's to be here.

## 5. Productivity

The funny thing about mindfulness is that people assume living in the present removes your drive to achieve your goals. The reverse is true. The more present I am, the more desire I feel to improve my life. And how do you improve your life? You already know it. I don't have to tell you that work is the only way to achieve things. Thinking about achieving your goals will not do anything real for you. Become a person who's productive *every day*. Make use of your time. Don't just waste it on watching tv, hanging out with your friends, gaming, or any other mindless routine activity. <u>Know how to get the most results in the least amount of time.</u> That's the ultimate aim of productivity skills.

# 6. Excellence

I half-assed many things in my life. "Let's just get it over with," was my motto. I was so <u>impatient</u> that I hardly did anything well. I just put in the minimum effort. Hence, I was never the best at anything. But then I realized that excellence is a skill. Look at Robert Greene who took 6 years to write another book. Or Lebron James who worked out during every off-season of his career. Or Helen Keller who published 5 books, despite being deaf and blind. But this is also true for successes that don't get attention in the media. Look at the top salesperson in any given organization who arrives early and leaves late every day. Or the mother who sacrifices nights out and dinner parties to raise her kid with all of her attention and love. That's called excellence.

# Chapter 11:

# 6 Ways To Transform Your Thinking

Changing your mindset isn't easy, but an open and positive attitude. Personal growth contributes to our choices to achieve physical, emotional, and spiritual well-being. Even something as simple as changing your mind can change your life. It's essential to take time for your mindset. During this period, we begin to understand ourselves, making us more compassionate and patient with ourselves. Our societies and cultures thrive in the professions that life brings to our lives and our tables. In this regard, the use of "bandage" solutions and rapid remedies to overcome certain obstacles in our lives have implications. These decisions never last long and are a matter of time and effort to slow down, ground up, and shift focus. Changing your mind means becoming more optimistic and giving your mind the breathing space, it needs to grow and expand. It's about looking at everything that doesn't work for you and being open to other methods that might help.

# 1. Practice Mindfulness

To adopt a more positive mindset, you must first recognize your current mindset. As you develop mindfulness, you can recognize and identify habituated thought patterns and then decide whether to use them or not. Mindfulness creates a distance between you and your thoughts, allowing you to see yourself separate from them. Incorporate mindfulness into your morning or evening routine and sit quietly for a few minutes (and practice gradually increasing the amount of time). When a thought comes to mind, turn your attention to your breathing instead of clinging to it.

# 2. Address Your Inner Critic

Your inner critic likes to convince you that it's not true, which often makes you feel pretty bad. Think of this voice as separate from you. Challenge the lie he is trying to feed you. Ask yourself. Is it true? Is there any evidence to support this claim? Another way is to thank this inner voice for their opinion and then say "no." I prefer not to fall into these negative thoughts. Alternatively, you may choose shorter, more direct answers, such as Not Now or Delete.

## 3. Know Your Triggers.

It is essential to be aware of certain people, situations, and situations to trigger more negative thoughts. Meeting your boss or making important life decisions can make you overly critical of yourself or question your worth. Once you become aware of your triggers, you can better prepare to control your thoughts than go back to your old negative thinking patterns. It is also helpful to see which cognitive biases, such as those mentioned above, recur most often.

## 4. Write It Out

Writing down your feelings on paper is a great way to relieve your thoughts and learn more about them. We often don't realize how harmful our thoughts are. Negative thinking patterns become habitual over time and usually go unnoticed. Taking notes makes it easier to identify areas that need attention. You can also ask questions as soon as they appear in the article to ensure they are accurate and relevant. If not, let them go or replace them with more positive thoughts. Writing in a diary, the first thing you do when you wake up in the morning is the perfect time to write down your stream of consciousness on paper.

## 5. Recite A Mantra

Shouting out a mantra or positive affirmation is a great way to break free from your current negative thoughts. When you feel that something negative is coming, you can make it a habit to recite or focus on it several times throughout the day. You can choose words or phrases that remind you to focus on the present and focus more on the positive.

## 6. Change Your Surroundings

Sometimes the thoughts are so loud that it is best to change the physical environment. Go for a walk, run or meet friends in nature. The point is to engage in something other than a negative cycle so you can get back to the problem when you're in a cleaner space. Choose your favourite activity or place, and you will feel better. If you need to be with others, have people around you to encourage you to think positively. (Avoid the trigger!)

Negative stereotypes of thoughts are challenging to break, especially when habituated. Patterns that have existed for years don't disappear overnight, so it's essential to show compassion and patience for yourself as you work.

# Chapter 12:

# Prepare For What's Coming

There are two types of people in this world, the ones who act and those who react! Some people know when to be ready and when to act. But others don't know anything about opportunity till the time they actually see the opportunity slipping away.

Opportunity and life have no reason to start and no reason to disappear. You were born, and you will be gone one day. But what you make up in this life will decide your ending and your memories in other people's minds. Opportunities come knocking on your door every now and then, and you rarely grab them. There are times when you barely know these moments, mostly after they have come and gone.

Mostly we are well aware of these moments because we are always looking out for them subconsciously. But how many times are we actually prepared to avail these moments? How often are we ready to grab these opportunities by the neck and mold them in whatever shape we want.

See, this is the difference between you and a successful person. A successful person would always be ready to avail themself of the first chance they get because they are always ready. They don't need time to get ready, gather all the tools, skills, or knowledge to pounce on every chance. Can you say the same thing about yourself?

If you want greatness in your life, you need to live differently. It would be best if you live prepared. It would be best if you lived like a hungry attentive lion. It is not always easy to stay alert and prepare for the worst. But you cannot always stay an idol just because life is uncertain.

There will be many moments in your life when you will feel like giving up because you were not ready enough. You will want to give up and start over again, and this is what any average person would do. But you are not an average person. There are opportunities all around you. If one thing brings you down, find a new one to lift you up.

If you think for one moment that it is too late to do something, this is the most stupid thing you have ever said to yourself. It is never too late to start anything. Your blessings await you. Every night your dreams should remind you what you need to achieve the next day. Every morning should be a warm-up for what task you are about to do today and end the day by doing it to its fullest.

Your weekends shouldn't be the time to relax but to work on what you did wrong throughout the week and what you are about to do the next week. You have control over your life as much as you control your own breathing. You can surely dictate your life on your own terms because, in the end, it will matter the most to you.

# Chapter 13:

# 7 Habits That Will Make You Successful

A man's habits are as good as his lifestyle. Some habits are akin to successful people. The path to greatness is less traveled and the habits to success may be difficult for some people to sustain.

The road to success is narrow and occasionally thorny because habits that will make you successful are uncomfortable and difficult to adapt. Similar to Charles Darwin's theory of survival for the fittest, only those who manage to trim their excesses and shape their habits will eventually be successful.

Here are seven habits that will make you successful:

## 1. Integrity

Integrity is one of the measures of success. It is the ability to live an honest life free from swindling, blackmail, and corruption among other vices. Integrity is the morality of a person and is relative from one person to another. However, there is a generally accepted threshold of integrity expected of people in different social, political, and economic classes.

Integrity is uncommon to most people making it highly valuable. People will forget how you looked but will never forget how you made them feel. Integrity holds back one from committing such awful mistakes. It will help you award the deserving, condemn vices, be intolerable to corruption, and make transparency your middle name.

The lack of integrity is responsible for the downfall of great people and business empires. Political leaders worldwide have lost their crown of glory to corruption. They were once the dream of every pupil in school and aspiring young leaders looked up to them. Corruption and greed stole that from them.

So powerful is integrity that successful people guard theirs' tooth and nail. Once eroded, their success is at stake. It may crumble down like a mound hill. Do you want to be successful? Have integrity.

## 2. An Open Mind

It is the ability to tolerate and be receptive to divergent ideas different from your beliefs. It takes a lot to accommodate the opinions of others and accept their reasoning to be rational. Successful people fully understand that they do not have a monopoly on brilliant ideas. As such, they cautiously welcome the proposals of other people while allowing room for further advancement.

Entertaining the ideas of other people does not mean blindly accepting them. It is the habit of successful people to be critical of everything, balancing their options and only settling for the best. An open mind translates to an analytical and inquisitive nature. The zeal to venture into the unknown and experiment with new waters.

Successful people are distinguished from others because they challenge the status quo. They seek to improve their best and develop alternatives to the existing routines. The reason why they are successful in the first place is their open mind.

How does one have an open mind? It is by being open to infinite possibilities of a hundred and one ways of approaching issues. Routine is an enemy of open-mindedness and by extension, success. It is of course inevitable not to follow a routine at our places of work, schools, or families. It is acceptable to that extent. Being its slave is completely unacceptable.

## 3. Move With Time

Time is never stagnant. The world evolves around time and seasons. The wise is he who deciphers and interprets them correctly. The measure of success in these modern times is different from those in the ancient days. A lot has changed.

In this era of technological advancements, we cannot afford to live in analog ways. The poor readers of seasons are stagnant in one position for a long time. Success is elusive in their hands. A look at business giants will reveal their mastery of times and seasons. They do not fumble at it. Not one bit.

Successful businesses deal with tools of the trade of the modern world. From the great Microsoft corporation to the Coca-cola company. All of them align themselves with the market demand presently. Learning the present time and season is a habit that will elevate you to success.

## 4.  <u>Learn From The Mistakes of Others</u>

It is prudent to learn from the mistakes of other people and not from yours. Keenly observe those ahead of you and watch out not to fall into their traps. It is regretful to be unable to take a cue from our predecessors and learn from their failures.

Successful people travel down roads once taken (for the advantage of hindsight) by others – except for a few adventurous ones who venture into the unknown. The benefit of hindsight is very important because we learn from the mistakes of those who preceded us and adjust accordingly.

Develop a habit of watching closely those ahead of you and take a cue from them not to commit similar mistakes. This habit will propel you to the doorstep of success.

## 5.  Investment Culture

It is prudent to be mindful of tomorrow. No amount of investment is too little. Successful people do not consume everything they produce. They save a portion of their income for the future. Investment is a culture developed over time. Some people find it difficult to postpone the entire consumption of their income. They will only settle when nothing is left. This is retrogressive.

An investment culture curbs wastage and emphasizes tomorrow's welfare. Moreover, to reduce risk, the investment portfolio is diversified. It is dangerous to risk everything in one endeavor. Captains of industries worldwide have invested broadly in different sectors. This makes them stay afloat even during tough economic seasons.

## 6.  Choosing Your Battles

On your way to success, do not make many enemies. This habit is ancient but very relevant to date. Unnecessary fights will wear you out and divert you away from the goal. Petty distractions will hijack your focus and successfully make you unsuccessful.

Learn to train your guns on things that matter. Feed your focus and starve your fears. Ignore useless petty issues that may lead to tainting of your public image. Fight your battles wisely.

## 7. Learn To Listen

Listening is an art beyond hearing. It is paying detailed attention to the speech of others, both verbal and non-verbal. Always listen more and talk less – a common argument for having two ears and one mouth. To be successful, you will have to pay closer attention to what is unspoken.

Listen to the way people communicate. You will pick up genuine intentions in their speech and align yourself accordingly.

Once perfected, these seven habits will make you successful.

# Chapter 14:

# 7 Habits To Change Your Life

Consistently, habit drives you to do what you do—regardless of whether it's a matter of considerations or conduct that happens naturally. Whatever that is, imagine a scenario where you could saddle the power of your habits to improve things. Envision a day-to-day existence where you have a habit for finishing projects, eating admirably, staying in contact with loved ones, and working to your fullest potential. At the point when you have an establishment of beneficial routines, you're setting yourself up for a full, sound, and effective life.

Here are 7 habits that Can change your entire life.

## 1. Pinpoint and Focus Entirely on Your Keystone Routine

Charles Duhigg, in his <u>power book</u> stipulates the essence of recognizing your Keystone Habit—the habit you distinguish as the main thing you can change about your life. To discover what that is for you, ask yourself, what continually worries you? Is it something you would that you like to stop, or something you would do and prefer not to begin? The cornerstone habit is distinctive for everybody, and it might take a couple of meetings of profound thought to pinpoint precisely what that habit is.

Whichever propensity you're chipping away at, pick each in turn. More than each in turn will be overpowering and will improve your probability of neglecting to improve any habits. Be that as it may, don't really accept that you can just change one thing about yourself; it's really the inverse. Dealing with this one Keystone Habit can have a positive gradually expanding influence into the remainder of your life also.

## 2. Recognize Your Present Daily Practice and the Reward You Get from It

Suppose you need to fabricate a habit for getting to the workplace a half hour early every day. You need to do this since you figured the extra peaceful time in the morning hours will assist you with being more gainful, and that profitability will be compensated by an expanded feeling of occupation fulfilment, and a generally speaking better workplace. As of now, you get to the workplace simply on schedule. Your present routine is to take off from your home in a hurry, at the specific time you've determined that (without traffic or episode) will get you to chip away at time. Your award is investing some additional energy at your home in the first part of the day, spending an additional half hour dozing or "charging your batteries" for the day ahead.

# 3. Take the Challenges Into Consideration

Challenges are regularly prompts that push you to fall once more into old habits. In the case of having to get to work earlier, your challenges may lie in your rest designs the prior night, or in organizing plans with a partner. These difficulties won't mysteriously vanish, so you need to consider them. In any case, don't let the presence of challenges, or stress that new difficulties will come up later on, discourage you from setting up your new propensities. In the event that your difficulties incorporate planning with others, make them a piece of your new daily practice, as I'll clarify later. At this moment, basically recognize what the difficulties or obstructions are.

# 4. Plan and Identifying Your New Routine

Old habits never vanish; they are basically supplanted with new propensities. In the case of getting to the workplace earlier, the new standard includes going out a half hour sooner. On the off chance that the old habit was remunerated with the possibility that you'll have more energy for the day by remaining in your home longer, the new propensity needs to centre around the possibility that more rest doesn't really mean more energy. All in all, you'll need to address what you think you'll be surrendering by supplanting the old habit.

## 5. Reinforce a 30 Days Challenge

By and large, your inability to minister beneficial routines basically comes from not adhering to them. A lot of studies show that habits, when performed day by day, can turn out to be important for your daily schedule in just 21 days. So set a beginning date and dispatch your game plan for a preliminary 30-day time span.

## 6. Empower Your Energy Through Setbacks

Here and there, it's not simply self-control that runs out. Now and then you are influenced from your ways by life "hindering" new objectives. In the event that something influences you from your test, the best game-plan is to assess the circumstance and perceive how you can get around, finished, or through that deterrent. Notwithstanding, when another propensity is set up, it really turns into our default setting. Assuming your standard habits are sound, unpleasant occasions are less inclined to lose you from your typical schedules. All in all, we're similarly prone to default to solid habits as we are to self-undermining habits, if those sound habits have become a piece of our ordinary daily practice.

# 7. Account Yourself and for Your Actions Publicly (Hold Yourself Accountable)

Your encouraging people are the most significant asset you will have at any point. Regardless of whether it's your closest companion, your accomplice or your Facebook posts, being responsible to somebody other than yourself will help you adhere to your objective. Simply remember that "responsible" isn't equivalent to "declaration". Anybody can advise the world they will rise ahead of schedule from here on out. However, on the off chance that that individual has a group of allies behind them, whom they routinely update, they are bound to stay with their new propensity during times when they are building up their new habit and inspiration is coming up short.

# Chapter 15:

# 7 Simple Tricks To Improve Your Confidence

So many successful people acclaim their self-esteem and confidence for their success. But few people explain how to build confidence or how to become confident. It's hard because confidence is built on different things, but it's built on choices and achievements that fuel your passions and make you happy and proud of who you are. Exploring these is one of the most enjoyable activities of your life.

Here are a few ways to start building your confidence:

## 1. Get Things Done

Confidence is built on achievement. If you achieve significant and small goals, you will feel much better. It starts with your daily goal. What do you need to accomplish today and every day of this week or three days this week to help you reach your goal? If you hit the goals you've set for yourself every day, you'll most likely start to hit weekly and monthly goals, bringing you closer to your semi-annual and annual goal ranges. Remember that progress is incremental, and significant changes don't happen overnight. You will feel like you can take on a big project and set yourself a lofty goal because you think you can achieve it. Set a goal and do it.

## 2. Monitor Your Progress

The best way to achieve your goals, big or small, is to break them down into smaller goals and track your progress. Whether you're trying to get a promotion, get a better job, go to college, change careers, eat healthier, or lose 10 pounds, the best way to know if you're making progress is to follow them. Try to quantify your accomplishments: how many job applications you apply for or go to college, what you eat and how much you exercise; write down any of your goals. It will keep you on track, and you will gain confidence in seeing your progress in real-time.

## 3. Do The Right Thing

The most confident people live by a value system and make decisions based on it, even when it's difficult and not necessarily in their best interest but in the greater good. Your actions and decisions define your personality. Ask yourself what the best version of yourself you would like to be and do it. Even if it's tough and it's the last thing you want to do, and it means a short-term sacrifice on your part, in the long run, you'll love yourself more and be more proud of who you are.

## 4. Exercise

In addition to benefiting your overall health, exercise helps maintain memory, improves concentration, helps manage stress, and prevents depression. It's hard to worry when you don't have excess energy to absorb, and besides being uncomfortable at times, exercise improves all aspects of your life. So stay active and make time to take care of yourself.

## 5. Be Fearless

Failure is not your enemy, and it is the fear of failure that paralyzes you. If you set big goals and dream big, you will feel overwhelmed and confident that you cannot achieve them. In times like these, you have to look inside yourself, gather every bit of courage you have, and keep going. All wildly successful people are afraid, and they keep working and taking risks because what they're trying to accomplish is more important and urgent than the fear of failure. Think about how much you want to achieve your goal, then put your worry aside and move on, one day at a time.

## 6. Follow Through

People respect people when they say they will do something, and they will do it. More importantly, you'll respect yourself if you say you'll do something and do it, and confidence will come more manageable because you know you don't mind the hard work. Actions give meaning to your words and will help pave the way for you to achieve your goals, strengthen relationships, and feel proud of who you are.

## 7. Do More of What Makes You Happy

What do you like to do in your spare time? Is it for hiking, kayaking, and enjoying the outdoors? Or do you live to lie on your sofa and watch all the great television available? Whatever you love, make space for it because life is short; you need time to enrich your life and rejuvenate yourself to be your best self.

# Chapter 16:

# 7 Ways On How To Expect Change For The Better In Your Life

The quicker you accept the fact that change is inevitable and can't be avoided, the better off you will be. The change could be better or worse; if you want it to be the former, you need to take complete control of your life. As life moves on, it's logical that the more transition and change you go through, the more opportunity you will have to perceive the patterns of your life, whether you will be able to handle the change or not, or how you can successfully negotiate and navigate these necessary transitions. We can do many things to turn our lives around; we can adopt habits and ideologies that will make us successful, but more importantly, happy. Now, you know yourself well enough to know what you want, what you realistically can do, and ideally, how you can accomplish those ideas and plans.

Here are some ways to expect change for the better in your life.

## 1. Find Meaning and Purpose

Finding meaning in your life is easier said than done. You need to understand that knowing one's specific purpose takes more time than one can imagine. Life does not always go according to our plan; there are loads of unexpected changes that we have to deal with on our way. Therefore, it is essential to understand the difference between goals and purposes; we often confuse these two. For example, you might think that your purpose is to become a famous athlete or scientist or even the president. However, these are merely your goals and not your purpose. Your purpose should be broader and more open than your ambitions or passions. It must positively impact the world or even be a key to your happiness and love.

## 2. Love and Respect Yourself

How can you expect to gain the respect and love of people when you can't even do that for yourself? To bring a positive evolution in your life, you need to build your self-confidence and self-esteem, which can only be achieved by working hard on yourself and taking action. Whether you face rejections or failures, accepting all the negativity and loving yourself regardless will help you move on more quickly. Putting yourself down and clinging to regrets will get you nowhere. As long as you love yourself and are satisfied with yourself, the opinions of others shouldn't matter to you.

## 3. Stop Making Excuses

This is a rule that you should embody in your soul; if you want to achieve something and bring positive change in your life, then you should stop lying to yourself. Understand that your time is limited, and the excuses you make will only waste it. Every explanation for failure is ultimately an excuse, and they do nothing but bring you down. Life isn't as easy as we see in the movies. Success and happiness can't be achieved in the blink of an eye. There will be many obstacles, and life will throw some serious curveballs at you. But what matters, in the end, is how we keep moving forward despite it all. Instead of making excuses and lying to ourselves for our failures, we should keep working hard.

## 4. Develop The Habit of Positive Thinking

It is said to believe that positive thoughts and confidence bring positive changes in our life. Sure, only thinking about it won't lead you to success, but it will motivate you and help you to give your absolute best. The law of attraction is proved to be somewhat true to many people. Therefore, we should try to be more optimistic and envision ourselves achieving our goals and working hard towards them. We should be in a positive mindset all the time; even if something negative happens to us, we should focus on the good more.

## 5.  Develop A Productive Routine

Having a productive routine is essential for a successful life; it is critical to manage your time wisely and eventually turn all the positive things into your habits. Start with smaller tasks, like making your bed after getting up. This can actually give you positive reinforcement to start your day and eventually lead to a happy and productive day.

## 6.  Set Goals For Yourself

You need to set some goals if you want to achieve anything worthwhile in your life. These goals are what keeps you motivated and helps you to stay on track. Set both short-term as well as long-term goals and work hard towards achieving them. Remember, your goals can change along the way; you have to be flexible about it and focus on giving your best effort in their pursuit.

## 7.  Live A Healthy Lifestyle

If your physical health is good, your mental health will be good, and vice versa. Adopting a healthier lifestyle can bring positive changes in your physical as well as mental health. It can help you turn your life around. It is essential to take care of our diet and make sure to exercise regularly. Good health is vital for a happy and content life.

## Conclusion

To sum it up, by following the above tips, you will have a tremendously positive result. You will be able to change your life for the better.

# Chapter 17:

# 7 Ways To Give A Great Presentation

While there are many different philosophies on how to give a presentation, there are a few simple skills you can learn to give excellent presentations, regardless of your preferred style. It can be helpful to set specific goals for yourself to improve over time. Many people spend their entire lives working on being a great speaker, so be patient and allow yourself to make mistakes.

In this article, we will discuss 7 ways you can begin learning and improving for your next presentation:

## 1. Keep Your Presentation Simple

When putting your presentation together, remember that simpler is better. Many presenters follow the "10-20-30" rule—use 10 or fewer slides, keep it under 20 minutes and make your font size at least 30 point. This framework ensures your presentation is clear, crisp and to the point. Much of the effectiveness of your presentation lies in your voice, explanations and body language, not the presentation materials themselves.

You should also try and keep your main ideas to three or fewer key points. Mention them at the beginning and end of your presentation to ensure the audience remembers the most important message.

## 2. Prepare and Practice

After you've put together your presentation, you should dedicate time to preparing your talking points. To do this, it can be helpful to ask a few trusted friends or colleagues to listen to a test run. Ask for their honest feedback about your visuals, speaking voice, body language and other aspects of the presentation.

Be sure to practice but not memorize your speech. If you memorize every line of your presentation, it can be easy to get off track when you are nervous or forget a word or two. Instead, prepare simple talking points that can direct your presentation. Speak openly and be confident in your knowledge on the subject.

## 3. Start Strong And Tell Stories

To capture your audience's attention throughout the presentation, it can be helpful to craft a strong, engaging beginning. However, you decide to start your presentation, make sure that it is relevant to your presentation and supports the main message you want your audience to remember at the end. Here are a few ways you can do this:

- Present an interesting question, problem, or anecdote.
- Quote an influential or interesting person.

- Share a story that leads to the main topic of your presentation.

- Show an interesting statistic, chart or image.

- Play a brief video that sets up your presentation.

- Make a statement that generates curiosity or shocks the audience.

Telling stories is a good way to make the concepts, ideas or information you are presenting relatable. It adds context and helps the audience more deeply understand and connect with your presentation. Again, only tell stories that will improve upon and support your main ideas.

## 4. Show Enthusiasm

Displaying your interest and care for the topic or information you are presenting will engage and capture the audience's attention. People enjoy listening to people who are genuinely excited about sharing their knowledge with others.

## 5. Find A Mentor or Mimic Other Inspirational Figures

While you should certainly develop and display your own speaking personality, it can be helpful to learn from other great speakers. Seek out someone at your company who you feel is a great presenter and ask them to be your mentor. Be clear about your goals and what you hope to gain from the relationship.

Also, there are nearly endless amounts of online videos, classes and other resources dedicated to improving presentation skills. Take time to study other presentations and mimic the qualities you find effective.

# 6. Use Visuals

If a concept can be supported or more easily explained with a visual aid, use them in your presentation. While you will likely have slides that will support your presentation visually, it can also help to have infographics, charts, photographs, videos, drawings or renderings. If it makes things difficult or more complex in any way, err towards keeping your presentation simple and accessible.

# 7. Support Your Audience

While you are creating and giving your presentation, be attentive to the needs of the audience by asking "What would make this learning experience the most enjoyable and effective possible?" This might mean explaining a difficult concept in more detail, moving around the stage, or inviting your audience to participate in some way.

Make sure you are honest and authentic throughout your presentation, connecting and being conversational with your audience. You should always talk "to" your audience instead of "at" them.

# Chapter 18:

# 8 Steps To Develop Beliefs That Will Drive you To Success

'Success' is a broad term. There is no universal definition of success, it varies from person to person considering their overall circumstances. We can all more or less agree that confidence plays a key role in it, and confidence comes from belief.

Even our most minute decisions and choices in life are a result of believing in some specific outcome that we have not observed yet.

However, merely believing in an ultimate success will not bring fortune knocking at your door. But it certainly can get you started—take tiny steps that might lead you towards your goal. Now, since we agree that having faith can move you towards success, let's look at some ways to rewire your brain into adopting productive beliefs.

Here are 8 Steps to Develop Beliefs That Will Drive You To Success:

## 1. Come Up with A Goal

Before you start, you need to decide what you want to achieve first. Keep in mind that you don't have to come up with something very specific right away because your expectations and decisions might change over time. Just outline a crude sense of what 'Achievement' and 'Success' mean to you in the present moment.

Begin here. Begin now. Work towards getting there.

## 2. Put Your Imagination Into Top Gear

"Logic will take you from A to B. Imagination will take you everywhere", said Albert Einstein.

Imagination is really important in any scenario whatsoever. It is what makes us humans different from animals. It is what gives us a reason to move forward—it gives us hope. And from that hope, we develop the will to do things we have never done before.

After going through the first step of determining your goal, you must now imagine yourself being successful in the near future. You have to literally picture yourself in the future, enjoying your essence of fulfilment as vividly as you can. This way, your ultimate success will appear a lot closer and realistic.

## 3. Write Notes to Yourself

Writing down your thoughts on paper is an effective way to get those thoughts stuck in your head for a long time. This is why children are encouraged to write down what is written in the books instead of memorizing them just by reading. You have to write short, simple, motivating notes to yourself that will encourage you to take actions towards your success. It doesn't matter whether you write in a notebook, or on your phone or wherever—just write it. On top of that, occasionally read what you've written and thus, you will remain charged with motivation at all times.

## 4. Make Reading A Habit

There are countless books written by successful people just so that they can share the struggle and experience behind their greatest achievements. In such an abundance of manuscripts, you may easily find books that portray narratives similar to your life and circumstances. Get reading and expand your knowledge. You'll get never-thought-before ideas that will guide you through your path to success. Reading such books will tremendously strengthen your faith in yourself, and in your success. Read what other successful people believed in—what drove them. You might even find newer beliefs to hold on to. No wonder why books are called 'Man's best friend'.

## 5. Talk To People Who Motivates You

Before taking this step, you have to be very careful about who you talk to. Basically, you have to speak out your goals and ambitions in life to someone who will be extremely supportive of you. Just talk to them about what you want, share your beliefs and they will motivate you from time to time towards success. They will act as powerful reminders. Being social beings, no human can ever reject the gist of motivation coming from another human being—especially when that is someone whom you can rely on comfortably. Humans have been the sole supporter of each other since eternity.

## 6. Make A Mantra

Self-affirming one-liners like 'I can do it', 'Nothing can stop me', 'Success is mine' etc. will establish a sense of firm confidence in your subconscious mind. Experts have been speculative about the power of our subconscious mind for long. The extent of what it can do is still beyond our grasp. But nonetheless, reciting subtle mantras isn't a difficult task.

Do it a couple of times every day and it will remain in your mind for ages, without you giving any conscious thought to it. Such subconscious affirmations may light you up in the right moment and show you the path to success when you least expect it.

## 7. Reward Yourself From Time To Time

Sometimes, your goals might be too far-fetched and as a result, you'll find it harder to believe in something so improbable right now. In a situation like this, what you can do is make short term objectives that ultimately lead to your main goal and for each of those objectives achieved, treat yourself with a reward of any sort—absolutely anything that pleases you. This way, your far cry success will become more apparent to you in the present time. Instant rewards like these will also keep you motivated and make you long for more. This will drive you to believe that you are getting there, you are getting closer and closer to success.

## 8. Having Faith In Yourself

Your faith is in your hands alone. How strongly you believe in what you deserve will motivate you. It will steer the way for self-confidence to fulfill your inner self. You may be extremely good at something but due to the lack of faith in your own capabilities, you never attempted it—how will you ever know that you were good at that? Your faith in yourself and your destined success will materialize before you through these rewards that you reserve for yourself. You absolutely deserve this!

## Final Thoughts

That self-confidence and belief and yourself, in your capabilities and strengths will make you work towards your goal. Keep in mind that whatever you believe in is what you live for. At the end of the day, each of us believed in something that made us thrive, made us work and move forward. Some believed in the military, some believed in maths, some believed in thievery—everyone had a belief which gave them a purpose—the purpose of materializing their belief in this world. How strongly you hold onto your belief will decide how successful you will become.

# Chapter 19:

# 8 Things Confident People Don't Do

True confidence is very different from egotistical swagger. When people believe in themselves and their abilities without bravado, there are certain things they simply don't do.

## 1. They Don't Make Excuses

If there's one trait confident people have in spades, it's <u>self-efficacy</u> -- the belief that they can make things happen. It's about having an internal locus of control rather than an external one. That's why you won't hear confident people blaming traffic for making them late or an unfair boss for their failure to get a promotion. Confident people don't make excuses, because they believe they're in control of their own lives.

## 2. They Don't Quit

Confident people don't give up the first time something goes wrong. They see both problems and failures as obstacles to overcome rather than impenetrable barriers to success. That doesn't mean, however, that they keep trying the same thing over and over. One of the first things confident people do when something goes wrong is to figure out why it went wrong and how they can prevent it the next time.

## 3. They Don't Wait For Permission To Act

Confident people don't need somebody to tell them what to do or when to do it. They don't waste time asking themselves questions like "Can I?" or "Should I?" If they ask themselves anything, it's "Why wouldn't I?" Whether it's running a meeting when the chairperson doesn't show up or going the extra mile to solve a customer's problem, it doesn't even occur to them to wait for somebody else to take care of it. They see what needs to be done, and they do it.

## 4. They Don't Seek Attention

People are turned off by those who are desperate for attention. Confident people know that being yourself is much more effective than trying to prove that you're important. People catch on to your attitude quickly and are more attracted to the right attitude than what, or how many, people you know. Confident people always seem to bring the right attitude. Confident people are masters of attention diffusion. When they're receiving attention for an accomplishment, they quickly shift the focus to all the people who worked hard to help get them there. They don't crave approval or praise because they draw their self-worth from within.

## 5. They Don't Need Constant Praise

Have you ever been around somebody who constantly needs to hear how great he or she is? Confident people don't do that. It goes back to that internal locus of control. They don't think that their success is dependent on other people's approval, and they understand that no matter how well they perform, there's always going to be somebody out there offering nothing but criticism. Confident people also know that the kind of confidence that's dependent on praise from other people isn't really confidence at all; it's narcissism.

## 6. They Don't Put Things Off

Why do people procrastinate? Sometimes it's simply because they're lazy. A lot of times, though, it's because they're afraid -- that is, afraid of change, failure or maybe even success. Confident people don't put things off. Because they believe in themselves and expect that their actions will lead them closer to their goals, they don't sit around waiting for the right time or the perfect circumstances. They know that today is the only time that matters. If they think it's not the right time, they make it the right time.

# 7. They Don't Pass Judgment

Confident people don't pass judgment on others because they know that everyone has something to offer, and they don't need to take other people down a notch in order to feel good about themselves. Comparing yourself to other people is limiting. Confident people don't waste time sizing people up and worrying about whether or not they measure up to everyone they meet.

# 8. They Don't Avoid Conflict

Confident people don't see conflict as something to be avoided at all costs; they see it as something to manage effectively. They don't go along to get along, even when that means having uncomfortable conversations or making unpleasant decisions. They know that conflict is part of life and that they can't avoid it without cheating themselves out of the good stuff, too.

Embracing the behaviours of confident people is a great way to increase your odds for success, which, in turn, will lead to more confidence. The science is clear; now you just have to decide to act on it.

# Chapter 20:

# 8 Ways To Adopt New Thoughts That Will Be Beneficial To Your Life

"Each morning we are born again. What we do today is what matters most." - Buddha

Is your glass half-empty or half-full? Answering this age-old question may reflect your outlook on life, your attitude toward yourself, whether you're optimistic or pessimistic, or it may even affect your health. Studies show that personality traits such as optimism and pessimism play a considerable role in determining your health and well-being. The positive thinking that comes with optimism is a practical part of stress management. Positive thinking in no way means that we keep our heads in the sand and ignore life's less pleasant situations. Instead, you have to approach the unpleasantness more positively and productively. Always think that something best is going to happen and ignore the worst-case scenarios.

Here are some ways for you to adopt new thoughts that will benefit your outlook on life.

## 1. Breaking Out Old Thinking Patterns

We all can get stuck in a loop of specific thoughts. Sure, they may look comfortable on the outside, but we don't realize that these thoughts are what's holding us back most of the time. It's crucial to let fresh ideas and thoughts into your life and break away from the negative ones to see new paths ahead. We could start by challenging our assumptions in every situation. We may already assume what's about to happen if we fall into some condition, but trying new preconceptions can open up some exciting possibilities for us.

## 2.  Rephrase The Problem

Your creativity can get limited by how you define or frame your problems. If you keep on looking at the problem from one side only, chances are you won't get much exposure to the solution. Whereas, if you look at it in different ways and different angles, new solutions can emerge. For example, the founder of Uber, Garret Camp, could have focused on buying and managing enough vehicles for him to make a profit. Instead, he looked more into how he could best entertain the passengers and thus, made a powerful app for their comfort.

## 3.  Think In Reverse

Try turning the problem upside-down if you're having difficulties finding a new approach. Flip the situation and explore the opposite of what you want to achieve. This can help you present innovative ways to tackle the real issue. If you're going to take a good picture, try all of its angles first so you can understand which grade will be more suitable and which angles you should avoid. If you want to develop a new design for your website, try its worst look first and then make it the exact opposite. Apply different types of creativity to tackle your problems.

## 4.  Make New Connections

Another way to generate new ideas and beneficial thoughts is by making unique and unexpected connections. Some of the best ideas click to you by chance, you hear or see something utterly unconnected to the situation you're trying to solve, and an idea has occurred to you almost instantly. For instance, architect Mick Pearce developed a groundbreaking climate-control system by taking the concept from the self-cooling mounds built by termites. You can pick on any set of random words, picture prompts, and objects of interest and then look for the novel association between them and your problem.

## 5.  Finding Fresh Perspectives

Adding extra dynamism to your thinking by taking a step back from your usual standpoint and viewing a problem through "fresh eyes" might be beneficial for you to tackle an issue and give new thoughts. You could also talk to someone with a different perspective, life experience, or cultural background and would be surprised to see their approach. Consider yourself being the other person and see life from their eyes, their point of view.

## 6.  Focus On The Good Things

Challenges and struggles are a part of life. When you're faced with obstacles, try and focus on the good part, no matter how seemingly insignificant or small it seems. If you keep looking for it, you will definitely find the proverbial silver lining in every cloud if it's not evident in the beginning.

## 7.  Practice Gratitude

Practicing gratitude is said to reduce stress, foster resilience, and improve self-esteem. If you're going through a bad time, think of people, moments, or things that bring you some kind of comfort and happiness and express your gratitude once in a while. This could be anything, from thanking your loved one to lending a helping hand to anyone.

## 8. Practice Positive Self-Talk

We sometimes are our own worst critics and tend to be the hardest on ourselves. This can cause you to form a negative opinion of yourself. This could be prevented by practicing positive self-talk. As a result, this could influence your ability to regulate your feelings, thoughts, and behaviors under stress.

## Conclusion

Developing a positive attitude can help you in many ways than you might realize. When you practice positive thinking, you consciously or subconsciously don't allow your mind to entertain any negative thoughts. You will start noticing remarkable changes all around you. By reducing your self-limiting beliefs, you will effectively grow as you have never imagined before. You can change your entire outlook on life by harnessing the power of positive thinking. You will also notice a significant boost in your confidence.

# Chapter 21:

# 8 Ways to Create A More Positive Mindset

Are you a glass-half-empty or half-full sort of person? Studies have demonstrated that both can impact your physical and mental health and that being a positive thinker is the better of the two.

A recent study followed 70,000 women from 2004 to 2012 and found that optimistic women had a significantly lower risk of dying from several major causes of death. Positive thinking isn't magic, and it will not suddenly make all your problems disappear; rather, what it will do is make those problems seem more manageable and help you approach these hardships productively and positively. We are going to list some things that will help you develop a positive mindset.

## 1. Focus On The Good Things

Challenging situations and obstacles are a part of life, but when you face such situations, you can focus on good things, whether they are small or big. When you try to look for it, you will find the silver lining, even if it is not immediately obvious. For example, if someone cancels plans, focus on how it frees up time for you to catch up on a TV show or other activity you enjoy

## 2. Practice Gratitude

Practicing gratitude has been shown to reduce stress, improve self-esteem, and foster resilience even in very difficult times. Think of people, moments, or things that bring you some kind of comfort or happiness and try to express your gratitude at least once a day. This can be thanking a co-worker for helping with a project, a loved one for washing the dishes, or your dog for the unconditional love they give you.

## 3. Keep A Gratitude Journal

Studies have found that writing down the things you're grateful for can improve your optimism and sense of well-being. You can do this by writing in a gratitude journal every day or jotting down a list of things you're grateful for on days you're having a hard time.

## 4. Open Yourself Up To Humor

Studies have found that laughter lowers stress, anxiety, and depression. It also improves coping skills, mood, and self-esteem.

Be open to humor in all situations, especially the difficult ones, and permit yourself to laugh. It instantly lightens the mood and makes things seem a little less difficult. Even if you're not feeling it, pretending or forcing yourself to laugh can improve your mood and lower stress.

## 5. Spend Time with Positive People

Negativity and positivity are contagious. Consider the people with whom you're spending time. Have you noticed how someone in a bad mood can bring down almost everyone in a room? A positive person has the opposite effect on others.

Being around positive people has been shown to improve self-esteem and increase your chances of reaching goals. Surround yourself with people who will lift you and help you see the bright side.

## 6. Practice Positive Self-Talk

We tend to be the hardest on ourselves and be our own worst critics. Over time, this can cause you to form a negative opinion of yourself that can be hard to shake. To stop this, you'll need to be mindful of the voice in your head and respond with positive messages, also known as positive self-talk.

Research shows that even a small shift in the way you talk to yourself can influence your ability to regulate your feelings, thoughts, and behavior under stress.

Here's an example of positive self-talk: Instead of thinking, "I really messed that up," try "I'll try it again a different way."

## 7. Identify Your Areas of Negativity

Take a good look at the different areas of your life and identify the ones in which you tend to be the most negative. Not sure? Ask a trusted friend or colleague. Chances are, they'll be able to offer some insight. A co-worker might notice that you tend to be negative at work. Your spouse may notice that you get especially negative while driving—tackle one area at a time.

I have found that writing down the things you're grateful for can improve your optimism and sense of well-being. You can do this by writing in a gratitude journal every day or jotting down a list of things you're grateful for on days you're having a hard time.

## 8. Start Every Day on A Positive Note

Create a ritual in which you start off each day with something uplifting and positive. Here are a few ideas:

- Tell yourself that it's going to be a great day or any other positive affirmation.
- Listen to a happy and positive song or playlist.
- Share some positivity by giving a compliment or doing something nice for someone.

# Chapter 22:

# 8 Ways To Deal With Setbacks In Life

Life is never the same for anyone - It is an ever-changing phenomenon, making you go through all sorts of highs and lows. And as good times are an intrinsic part of your life, so are bad times. One day you might find yourself indebted by 3-digit figures while having only $40 in your savings account. Next day, you might be vacationing in Hawaii because you got a job that you like and pays $100,000 a year. There's absolutely no certainty to life (except passing away) and that's the beauty of it. You never know what is in store for you. But you have to keep living to see it for yourself. Setbacks in life cannot be avoided by anyone. Life will give you hardships, troubles, break ups, diabetes, unpaid bills, stuck toilet and so much more. It's all a part of your life.

Here's 8 ways that you might want to take notes of, for whenever you may find yourself in a difficult position in dealing with setback in life.

## 1. Accept And If Possible, Embrace It

The difference between accepting and embracing is that when you accept something, you only believe it to be, whether you agree or disagree. But when you embrace something, you truly KNOW it to be true and accept it as a whole. There is no dilemma or disagreement after you have embraced something.

So, when you find yourself in a difficult situation in life, accept it for what it is and make yourself whole-heartedly believe that this problem in your life, at this specific time, is a part of your life. This problem is what makes you complete. This problem is meant for you and only you can go through it. And you will. Period. There can be no other way.

The sooner you embrace your problem, the sooner you can fix it. Trying to bypass it will only add upon your headaches.

## 2.  Learn From It

Seriously, I can't emphasize how important it is to LEARN from the setbacks you face in your life. Every hardship is a learning opportunity. The more you face challenges, the more you grow. Your capabilities expand with every issue you solve—every difficulty you go through, you rediscover yourself. And when you finally deal off with it, you are reborn. You are a new person with more wisdom and experience.

When you fail at something, try to explore why you failed. Be open-minded about scrutinizing yourself. Why couldn't you overcome a certain situation? Why do you think of this scenario as a 'setback'? The moment you find the answers to these questions is the moment you will have found the solution.

## 3. Execute What You Have Learnt

The only next step from here is to execute that solution and make sure that the next time you face a similar situation, you'll deal with it by having both your arms tied back and blindfolded. All you have to do is remember what you did in a similar past experience and reapply your previous solution.

Thomas A. Edison, the inventor of the light bulb, failed 10,000 times before finally making it. And he said "I have not failed. I just found 10,000 ways that won't work".

The lesson here is that you have to take every setback as a lesson, that's it.

# 4. Without Shadow, You Can Never Appreciate Light

This metaphor is applicable to all things opposite in this universe. Everything has a reciprocal; without one, the other cannot exist. Just as without shadow, we wouldn't have known what light is, similarly, without light, we could've never known about shadow. The two opposites identify and complete each other.

Too much of philosophy class, but to sum it up, your problems in life, ironically, is exactly why you can enjoy your life. For example, if you are a chess player, then defeating other chess players will give you enjoyment while getting defeated will give you distress. But, when you are a chess prodigy—you have defeated every single chess player on earth and there's no one else to defeat, then what will you do to derive pleasure? Truth is, you can now no longer enjoy chess. You have no one to defeat. No one gives you the fear of losing anymore and as a result, the taste of winning has lost its appeal to you.

So, whenever you face a problem in life, appreciate it because without it, you can't enjoy the state of not having a problem. Problems give you the pleasure of learning from them and solving them.

## 5. View Every Obstacle As An Opportunity

This one's especially for long term hindrances to your regular life. The COVID-19 pandemic for instance, has set us back for almost two years now. As distressing it is, there is also some positive impact of it. A long-term setback opens up a plethora of new avenues for you to explore. You suddenly get a large amount of time to experiment with things that you have never tried before.

When you have to pause a regular part of your life, you can do other things in the meantime. I believe that every one of us has a specific talent and most people never know what their talent is simply because they have never tried that thing.

## 6. Don't Be Afraid To Experiment

People pursue their whole life for a job that they don't like and most of them never ever get good at it. As a result, their true talent gets buried under their own efforts. Life just carries on with unfound potential. But when some obstacle comes up and frees you from the clutches of doing what you have been doing for a long time, then you should get around and experiment. Who knows? You, a bored high school teacher, might be a natural at tennis. You won't know it unless you are fired from that job and actually play tennis to get over it. So whenever life gives you lemons, quit trying to hold on to it. Move on and try new things instead.

## 7. Stop Comparing Yourself To Others

The thing is, we humans are emotional beings. We become emotionally vulnerable when we are going through something that isn't supposed to be. And in such times, when we see other people doing fantastic things in life, it naturally makes us succumb to more self-loathing. We think lowly of our own selves, and it is perfectly normal to feel this way. Talking and comparing ourselves to people who are seemingly untouched by setbacks is a counterproductive move. You will listen to their success-stories and get depressed—lose self-esteem. Even if they try their best to advise you, it won't get through to you. You won't be able to relate to them.

## 8. Talk To People Other People Who Are Having Their Own Setbacks In Life

I'm not asking you to talk to just any people. I'm being very specific here: talk to people who are going through bad times as well.

If you start talking to others who are struggling in life, perhaps more so compared to you, then you'll see that everyone else is also having difficulties in life. It will seem natural to you. Moreover, having talked with others might even show you that you are actually doing better than all these other people. You can always find someone who is dealing with more trouble than you and that will enlighten you. That will encourage you. If someone else can deal with tougher setbacks in life, why can't you?

Besides, listening to other people will give you a completely new perspective that you can use for yourself if you ever find yourself in a similar situation as others whom you have talked with.

## Conclusion

Setbacks are a part of life. Without them we wouldn't know what the good times are. Without them we wouldn't appreciate the success that we have gotten. Without them we wouldn't cherish the moments that got us to where we are heading to. And without them there wouldn't be any challenge to fill our souls with passion and fire. Take setbacks as a natural process in the journey. Use it to fuel your drive. Use it to move your life forward one step at a time.

# Chapter 23:

# 8 Ways to Discover What's Holding You Back From Achieving Your Visions

We all have dreams, and I have no questions; you have made attempts at seeking after your goals. Oh, as a general rule, life's battles get the better of you and keep you down. The pressure of everyday life, again and again, puts you down. Regardless of your determination, devotion, and want, alone, they are not enough.

Being here exhibits you are not able to settle for a mediocre life and hidden desires. To help you in your goal of seeking after your objectives, you must become acquainted with those things keeping you down. When you do, you will want to eliminate every single reason keeping you down.

## 1. Fear

The deep-rooted foe is very likely a critical factor in keeping many of you from seeking after your objectives. It prevents you from acting, making you scared of venturing out. Dread is the thing that keeps you down.

Dread is one reason why we don't follow what we truly need throughout everyday life.

• Fear of disappointment

• Fear of dismissal

• Fear of mocking

• Fear of disappointment

Quit allowing your feelings of fear to keep you down!

## 2. Procrastination

Putting things off till the following week, one month from now, one year from now, and regularly forever. You're not exactly sure the thing you're hanging tight for, but rather when whatever it happens, you'll be prepared to start seeking after your objectives. Be that as it may, this day never comes. Your fantasy stays as just a fantasy. Putting things off can just keep you down.

Quit allowing your Procrastination to keep you down!

## 3. Justifications

Do you find yourself procrastinating and making excuses for why you can't start working toward your goals? Those that succeed in accomplishing their objectives can overcome obstacles. So many individuals make excuses for themselves, believing they can't achieve a better career, start their own business, or find their ideal lifemate.

- It isn't the correct time

- I am insufficient

- I am too old/young

Don't allow your excuses to hold you back any longer!

## 4. Lack of Confidence

Lack of confidence in yourself or your ability to achieve your goals will inevitably hold you back. Our actions, or lack thereof, are influenced by what goes on in our subconscious mind. We have self-limiting and negative beliefs that may be preventing us from enjoying an extraordinary life.

Nothing will be able to stop you if you believe in yourself. Bringing your limiting beliefs into focus will help you achieve your objectives.

Don't let your lack of confidence keep you back!

## 5. There Isn't A Big Picture

Others refer to what I call a breakthrough goal as a BHAG - Big Hairy Audacious Goal. A goal is what you need to keep you motivated and drive you to achieve it every day. Start small and dream big. You'll need a strong enough passion to propel you forward. Your ambitions will not motivate you until you first dream big.

For your objectives to be beneficial to you, they must assist you in realizing your ambitions. Those lofty ambitions. Goals can only motivate you, help you stay focused, and help you make the adjustments you need to make, as well as provide you the fortitude to overcome difficulties as you chase your big-picture dreams if they matter to you.

Stop allowing your big picture to stifle your progress!

## 6. Inability To Concentrate

Your chances of success are slashed every moment you lose focus. When we spread our focus too thin, we dilute our effort and lose the ability to focus on the most significant tasks. When you're pulled in a lot of different directions and have a lot of conflicting priorities fighting for your attention, it's easy to lose track of what's important. Any attempts to achieve vital goals will be harmed as a result of this.

Stop allowing your lack of concentration to keep you back!

## 7. Failure to Make a Plan

Finally, if you don't have a strategy, it's easy to become lost along the route. Consider driving across the country without a map, say from London to Glasgow. While you have a rough route in mind, there are many lands to cover and a lot of false turns and dead ends to be avoided.

You can get there with the help of a GPS. It plots your path and creates a plan for you. A plan provides you with the road map you need to reach your objectives. This is the process of determining what you need to accomplish to reach your objectives. This is where you put in the time and effort to write out a plan of the steps you need to follow, the resources you'll need, and the amount of time you'll need to invest.

Stop allowing the lack of a strategy holds you back!

## 8. Not Keeping Track of Your Progress and Making Necessary Modifications

Goals, by their very nature, take time to attain. Therefore, it's critical to keep track of your progress. You won't know what's working and what's not if you don't get quick and actionable feedback. You won't be able to tell when to alter or when to keep doing what you're doing. Anyone who is continuously successful in accomplishing their goals also reviews their goals and progress regularly. Regularly reviewing your goals allows you to make early modifications to stay on track.

Stop allowing not reviewing and adjusting your progress to hold you back!

# Chapter 24:

# 9 Habits of Successful Students

Successful students are made up of a common DNA. This is because they share a backbone – their success. In the words of Aristotle, *we are what we repeatedly do. Excellence, then, is not an act, but a habit.* Success is a habit that this clique of students has perfected meticulously.

Here are 9 habits of successful students:

## 1. They Identify With Their Status

It begins at the beginning. It is a paradox in itself. The start of the success of successful students (pun intended) is their acceptance that they are students of whatever discipline they are pursuing. When they correctly identify with their discipline, the journey begins.

Next, they identify with the institution/person under whose tutelage they are placed. Appreciating the expertise of their seniors is as important as it is that they are successful. No one crowns himself King; Kingmakers do crown him or her. In this case, the institution provides the opportunity for the student and teacher to meet.

Successful students, at all levels, identify with their centers of learning. Be it primary school, high school, technical-vocational colleges, or universities, successful students are proud of them (at least during the duration of their study).

## 2. They Have A Good Attitude

How does the attitude of students connect with their success? Again, why are successful students proud of where they learn? If they have a bad attitude towards their centers of learning, they will dislike their teachers – those responsible for imparting knowledge to them. As a result, whatever they learn will not stick.

Successful students are as good as their attitude is towards their teachers, institutions, and discipline of study. If you want to master your studies then change your attitude. A good attitude opens you up to greater possibilities. The possibilities that will be open to you are infinite.

## 3. They Relate Well With Their Tutors

The relationship between learners and their teachers should strictly be professional (there is the risk of unethical behavior if it crosses that line). When learners are in harmony with their tutors, learning is easier.

A good relationship between students and teachers breeds trust. Trust is the foundation upon which success is founded. The goodwill of both the teacher and the student is based on the relationship between them. The former being devoted to the latter's needs and the latter submissive to the former's instructions.

Ask top candidates of national examinations how their relationship with their teachers was and you will hear of nothing short of "the best."

## 4. They Are Willing To Go The Extra Mile

The story of successful students is akin to a fairytale in a fairyland. The prince does everything to protect his bride. He will go the extra mile to make her happy, to know her better, and even to cheer her up. With this infinite love, either of them is ready to move mountains for the sake of the other.

Successful students and their studies are like the groom and bride in the fairyland. The students do not mind going an extra mile for their bride (studies). They study late into the night, sacrifice their free time to grasp new concepts, and are even ready to forego short-time pleasures for the sake of their education.

This sacrifice is what distinguishes them from the rest of their peers.

## 5. They Are Inquisitive

Successful students are always curious about what they do not know. The unknown stirs curiosity in them; they are never content with the status quo. Their inquisitive nature is gold – a rare characteristic in most students. A majority of them are satisfied with what they know.

Their inquisitiveness births innovation. While settling for nothing short of the best, they try out new practices, re-design existing models and create new inventions. They stand out from their peers. Being inquisitive is not disrespect for authority or existing knowledge. On the contrary, it is appreciating the current principles and building on them to come up with something better.

## 6.  They Have Focus

Their primary goal is clear and everything else is secondary. Successful students have a razor-sharp focus of the eagle, not distracted by anything that crosses their line.

A perfect real-life example is that of a hunting lion. When it settles on its prey from a herd, it chases it to the end. It can even pass other animals while chasing the specific target. The lion does not care whether the animal that crosses its path is better than its target. The only thing that matters is getting to its target.

When students decide to prioritize their education above any other interest, their energy and concentration are drawn to it. Success will be their cup of tea.

## 7.  They Do Their Due Diligence

The art of assuming is foreign to successful students. They treat everything in their discipline with utmost care. They research on results of experiments and answer the whys that arise.

It is never said by their tutors that they neglected their duty of research. Successful students know their role and they play it well. They know where and when to stop. This makes them disciplined compared to their colleagues.

Their discipline is outstanding. Shape your discipline and you will join the exclusive club of successful students.

## 8.  Abide By The Book

Successful students stick to the rules of the game. This is important since it is not all students who manage to complete the race. Like any other commitment, learning requires agility. It has its own rules, the common and the silent rules. Most important are the unspoken rules that students are expected to abide by.

What is left unsaid, for example, is that students are not expected to be in romantic relationships because it will get in the way of their education.

## 9.  They Are Punctual

Successful students keep time. Punctuality is the backbone of planning which is very important for focused people. Keeping time helps students avoid missing classes and group discussions or arriving very late for the same.

Success itself arrives punctually in the sense that it gives proportionate results to the input invested by those who court it. Successful students are the best timekeepers. Those who do not observe time have learned the hard way how to.

These 9 habits are what successful students do to make it to the top and stay there.

# Chapter 25:

# 9 Habits of Highly Successful People

*Success comes to people who deserve it.* I bet you have heard this statement quite a few times, right? So, what does it mean exactly? Does it mean that you are either born worthy or unworthy of success? Absolutely not. Everyone is born worthy, but the one thing that makes some people successful is their winning habits and their commitment to these habits.

Today, we will learn how to master ten simple habits and behaviors that will help you become successful.

## 1. Be an Avid Learner

If you didn't know, almost all of the most successful people in the world are avid learners. So, do not shy away from opportunities when it comes to learning. Wake up each day and look forward to learning new things, and in no time, I bet you will experience how enriching it really is. Also, learning new things has the effect of revitalizing a person. So, if you want to have more knowledge to kickstart your journey in the right direction, here are some things that you can do - make sure to read, even if it is just a page or two, daily. It could be anything that interests you. I personally love reading self-help books. If you are not that much of a reader, you can even listen to a podcast, watch an informative video, or sign up for a course. Choose what piques your interest, and just dive into it!

## 2. Failure is the Pillar of Success

Most people are afraid to delve into something new, start a new chapter of their lives, and chase after their dreams – all because they are scared to fail. If you are one of those people who are scared to fail, well, don't be! Because what failure actually does is prepares you to achieve your dream. It just makes sure that you are able to handle the success when you finally have it. So, when you accept that failure is an inevitable part of your journey, you will be able to plan the right course of action to tackle it instead of just being too scared to move forward. Successful people are never scared of failure; They just turn it around by seeing it as an opportunity to learn.

## 3. Get Up Early

I bet you have heard this a couple of thousand times already! But whoever told you so was not lying. Almost all successful individuals are early risers! They say that starting the morning right ensures a fruitful day ahead. It is true! Think about it, on the day you get up early, you feel a boost of productivity as compared to when you wake up late and have to struggle against the clock. You will have plenty of time and a good mood to go through the rest of the day which will give you better outcomes. All you have to do is set up a bedtime reminder. This is going to make sure that you enough rest to get up in the morning instead of snoozing your alarm on repeat! Not a morning person? Don't worry. I have got you covered! Start slow and set the alarm 15 minutes before when you usually wake up. It doesn't sound like much, eh? But trust me, you will be motivated to wake up earlier when you see how much difference 15 minutes can make to your day.

## 4. Have Your Own Morning Ritual

Morning rituals are the most common habit among achievers. It will pump you up to go through the day with a bang! You just have to make a routine for yourself and make sure to follow it every day. You can take inspiration from the morning routines of people you look up to but remember it has to benefit you. So, you might be wondering, *what do I include in the ritual?* I would suggest you make your bed first thing in the morning. This might not sound as great a deal, but hey, it is a tested and approved method to boost your productivity. It is even implemented in the military. Doing this will motivate you as you get a sense of achievement as you have completed a task as soon as you woke up. After that, it could be anything that will encourage you, such as a walk, a workout session, reading, journaling, or meditating.

# 5. Stop Procrastinating

From delaying one task to not keeping up with your deadlines, procrastination becomes a deadly habit. It becomes almost unstoppable! Did you know, most people fail to achieve their dreams even if they have the potential just because of procrastination? Well, they do. And you might not want to become one of them. They say, "Old habits die hard," true, but they do die if you want them to. Procrastination has to be the hardest thing we have to deal with, even though we hey created it in the first place. Trust me, I speak from experience!

So what do you do to stop this? Break your task into small bite-sized pieces. Sometimes, it is just the heaviness of the task that keeps us from doing it. Take breaks in between to keep yourself motivated.

Another thing that you can do is the "minute rule." Divide your tasks by how much time they take. The tasks that take less than 5 minutes, you do it right then. Then you can bigger tasks into small time frames and complete them. Make sure you do not get too lost in the breaks, though!

# 6. Set Goals

I cannot even begin to tell you how effective goal setting is. A goal gives you the right direction and motivation. It also gives you a sense of urgency to do a task that is going to just take your productivity level from 0 to 10 in no time!

So how do you set goals? Simple. Think about the goals you want to achieve and write them down. But make sure that you set realistic goals. If you find it difficult, don't worry. Start small and slow. Start by making a to-do list for the day. You will find out soo that the satisfaction in ticking those off your list is unbelievable. It will also drive you to tick more of them off!

## 7.   Make Your Health a Priority

Health is Wealth. Yes, it is a fact! When you give your body the right things and make it a priority, it gives you back by keeping you and your mind healthy. I bet you've heard the saying "You are what you eat," and by "eat," it does not simply mean to chew and swallow! It also means that you need to feed your body, soul, and mind with things you want them to be like. Read, listen, learn, and eat healthy. You could set a goal to eat clean for the week. Or workout at least for 10 minutes. And see for yourself how it gives you the energy to smash those goals you've been holding off! Also, great news – you can have cheat days once a week!

## 8.   Plan Your Day the Night Before

"When you fail to plan, you plan to fail." People who succeed in life are not by mere coincidence or luck. It is the result of detailed, focused planning. So, you need to start planning your way to success too. Before you sleep tonight, ask yourself, *What is the most important thing that I have to do tomorrow?* Plan what assignments, meetings, or classes you have to complete. Planning ahead will not only make you organized and ready, it also highly increases your chances to succeed. So, don't forget to plan your day tonight!


## 9. Master the Habit Loop

Behavioral expert, BJ Fogg, explains that habits are formed around three elements: Cue, Routine, and Reward. Cue is the initial desire that motivates your behavior. Routine is the action you take. And the reward is the pleasure you gain after completion. So why am I telling you all of this? Because this habit loop is how we are wired. It is what motivates us. We seek pleasure and avoid pain. And you can use this loop to your advantage! Let's say you want to finish an assignment. Think of the reason why you want to. Maybe you don't want to fall behind someone or want to impress someone. It could be anything! Now time for you to set your rewards. It could be eating a slice of cheesecake or watching an episode of your favorite series after you've finished. Rewards motivate you when you slack off. Play around until you find a combination that works best for you. You will also need a cue; it could be anything like a notification on your phone, an email, or simply your desire. You can set a cue yourself by creating a reminder.

Habits are what make a man. I hope you follow these habits and start your journey the right way to becoming successful in life

# Chapter 26:

# 10 Habits of Unsuccessful People

Highly successful people (in any of the many ways that "success" can be defined) seem to recognize a few basic principles. The most important of these is that your energy, not your time, is restricted each day and must be carefully controlled.

Here are 10 of the most popular self-imposed blocks that have a troll on your success. If you come across one, use it as a cue to reevaluate, reflect, and change direction.

### 1. Worry of the Most Unlikely Outcome

Despite its label as a "maladaptive trait," worrying has an evolutionary connection to intelligence. This is why, according to Jeremy Coplan, lead author of a study published of Frontiers in Evolutionary Neuroscience, effective people are naturally nervous.

Whatever the case may be, to work correctly, you must be able to distinguish between which fears are worth reacting to and which are your brain's attempt to "prepare" you for survival by conjuring up the most severe possible risk. This is an antiquated, animalistic mechanism that is useless in everyday life. Highly effective people should not spend their time worrying about the things that are least likely to happen.

## 2. Just Talking the Talk

"I'm preparing to do this and that." What's better than announcing on social media that you're starting a business? Putting it into action.

Entrepreneur Derek Sivers argued in his 2010 TED talk, "Keep Your Goals to Yourself," that disclosing your intentions can be detrimental rather than inspiring. People will sometimes applaud you just for stating your purpose, he said, and this applause, ironically, may drain your motivation to carry out the plans you've just outlined.

"Psychotherapists have discovered that telling others your goal and having them embrace it is known as a 'social reality,'" Sivers explained in his talk. "The mind is deceived into believing it has already been accomplished. Then, after you've had your satisfaction, you're less likely to put in the necessary effort."

There's nothing wrong with expressing your happiness. However, try to keep your mouth shut before you have good news, not just good intentions.

**3.** Ruminating and Not Doing Anything About It.

Reflecting becomes ruminating as the intention to act dissolves in favor of constantly replaying certain situations or issues through your mind. Self-awareness is common among highly successful individuals, or at least it should be. This means they devote a significant amount of time to reflecting on their behavior and experiences and determining how they can change. However, they do not waste mental energy pondering what went wrong rather than consciously modifying what needs to be changed to fix the issue.

## 4. Choosing the Wrong People To Spend Time With

The people you hang out with can either inspire you to be your best self or bring out your worst traits. Spend time with people who can motivate you to make the changes you want to make in your life. Do you want to fail at that goal completely? If it's the case, spend time with people who gloat about their bad habits. People get their energy from each other. Always remember that you are the average of the 5 people that you spend most of your time with.

## 5. Being Resentful for Taking Time for Themselves

People who have experienced any degree of success understand that it is a multi-faceted operation. You won't be able to work at your best if you're tired, undernourished, or experiencing some other sort of extreme imbalance in your life.

As a result, highly successful individuals are just as dedicated to relaxation and health as work and efficiency. They don't stress themselves up about how much they should have done in a three-day weekend or why they shouldn't take time off when they need it.

## 6. Constantly Concentrating on the Negative

It's mind-boggling to focus on the negative aspects of life because it'll only make you feel worse. You don't have to believe that life is simple to concentrate on the positive. You should maintain a rational viewpoint without always pointing out the flaws in everything you see.

We've all met someone who is still complaining about something. "Ugh, it rained this morning, and my shoes were soaked through and through." Yes, that's a disappointment. You won't be able to affect the weather, unfortunately. You should put on a new pair of shoes if you want to.

It's fine if you're having a rough day; we're all irritable at times; everybody gets irritable now and then. However, you are living a poor life if you despise anything. That's what there is to it.

## 7. Justifying Their Place in Life

Taking on exceptional work also elicits questions and, at times, judgments from those who don't believe in your project or are suspicious of its long-term viability. Constantly feeling the need to explain or justify your role in life, on the other hand, is not only exhausting but also unnecessary. Highly effective people understand that you can't get approval from people who don't want it.

## 8. Allowing Themselves To Be Sucked Into a State of Laziness

We've all had times when we've been compelled to cancel plans. Leaving the house, even for something "fun," can feel like a Herculean task at times.

However, it is fresh and novel experiences that make life so beautiful. You aren't fully involved in your own life when you succumb to laziness, which is unfair to your friends, family, spouse, and those who want to share it with you.

# 9. Worrying That Isn't Essential and Unregulated Thought Patterns

Worrying is among the most common ways people drain their energy doing. It is the act of anticipating the worst-case scenario and assuming that it is not only probable but most likely.

Worrying does not make you more equipped to deal with life's challenges instead, it makes you more likely to build your fears. You'd be surprised to learn that 99.9% of your worries were baseless and never "came true" if you made a list of everything you've ever worried about in your life.

If you just made a list of everything you didn't care about in life, you'd find that worrying didn't change anything; it just sapped your energy at the moment. The only thing it has done for you is that it made things more complicated, twisted, and less fun. It is not only ineffective, but completely pointless as well. Highly successful people learn to concentrate on something else rather than spend their time worrying about what could go wrong.

# 10. There Is Just Too Much Optimistic Thought

It's self-evident that no one achieves remarkable success without first confronting destructive thought patterns. What's less evident is that highly successful people don't partake in excessive positive thinking, which can be arbitrary, distorted, and even distracting in excess. Worse, they set themselves up for failure or disappointment by thinking too positively. Instead, highly successful people understand the power of neutral thought, which means they don't try to make life into something.

## Conclusion

If you don't want to be an unsuccessful person, you need to make a conscious effort to avoid doing these things. Focus on the habits that would bring you positive change instead, which we will discuss in another segment.

# Chapter 27:

# 10 Habits to Change Your Life

I'm sure everyone wonders at a certain point in their life that what is the thing that is stopping them from reaching their goals. It is your bad and unhealthy habits that hold you down. If you want to succeed in life, you need to get rid of these habits and adopt healthy habits to help you in the long run.

Here are 10 healthy habits that will change your life completely if you can adopt them in your daily life:

## 1. Start Following a Morning Ritual

Everyone has something that they love to do, i.e., things that boost their energy and uplifts their mood. Find one for yourself and do that every morning. It will help you kickstart your day with a bright and cheerful mood. It will also help you to eliminate mental fatigue and stress. You will find yourself super energetic and productive. Let me tell you some morning rituals that you can try and get benefitted from.

- *Eating Healthy:* If you are very passionate about health and fitness, eating healthy as a morning ritual might be a win-win situation for you. You can have a nutritious breakfast every morning. Balance your breakfast with proper amounts of carbs, fats, proteins, etc. It will not only help you in staying healthy but will also help you kickstart your day on a proactive note.

- *Meditating:* Meditation is an excellent way of clearing your mind, enhancing your awareness, and improving your focus. You can meditate for 20 to 30 minutes every morning. Then you can take a nice warm shower, followed by a fresh cup of coffee. Most importantly, meditating regularly will also help you strengthen your immune system, promote emotional stability, and reduce stress.

- *Motivating:* A daily dose of motivation can work wonders for you. When you are motivated, your productivity doubles, and you make the best out of your day. Every morning, you can simply ask yourself questions like, "If it is the last day of your life, what do you want to do?", "What productive thing can I do today to make the best out of the day" "What do I need to do in order to avoid regretting later for having wasted a day?". When you ask yourself questions like these, you are actually instructing your brain to be prepared for having a packed-up and productive day.

- *Writing:* Writing can be a super-effective way of kickstarting your day. When you journal all your thoughts and emotions every day after waking up, it allows you to relieve yourself from all the mental clutter, unlocks your creative side, and sharpens your focus.

- ***Working Out:*** Working out is a great morning ritual that you can follow every day. When you work out daily, it helps you burn more fat, improves your blood circulation, and boosts your energy level. If you are interested in fitness and health, this is the perfect morning ritual for you. You can do some cardio exercises, or some strength training, or both. Depending on your suitability, create a workout routine for yourself and make sure to stick to that. If you don't stick to your routine, it won't be of much help.

## 2. Start Following the 80/20 Rule

The 80/20 rule states that almost 20% of the tasks you perform are responsible for yielding 80% of the results. It is why you should invest more time in tasks that can give you more significant results instead of wasting your time on tasks that yield little to no results. In this way, you can not only save time but also maximize your productivity. Most importantly, when you see the results after performing those tasks, you will be more motivated to complete the following tasks. After you have finished performing these tasks, now you can quickly move your concentration and focus towards other activities that you need to do throughout your day.

## 3. Practice Lots of Reading

Reading is a great habit and a great way to stimulate your creativity and gaining more knowledge. When you get immersed in reading, it calms you and improves your focus, almost similar to meditating. If you practice reading before going to bed, you are going to have a fantastic sleep. You can read non-fiction books, which will help you seek motivation, develop new ideas, and broaden your horizon. You can also get a lot of advice about how to handle certain situations in life.

## 4. Start Single-tasking

Multitasking is hard, and almost 2% of the world's total population can do this properly. You can try multitasking occasionally. If you keep on trying to do this all the time, it will form a mental clutter, and as a result, your brain won't be able to filter out unnecessary information. Many studies have suggested that it can severely damage your cognitive control and lower your efficiency when you multitask a lot. It is the main reason why you should try to do single tasking more than multitasking. Prepare a list of all the tasks you need to perform in a day and start with the most important one. Make sure not to rush and to complete one thing at a time.

## 5. Start Appreciating More

Appreciating things is totally dependent on your mentality. For example, some people can whine and complain about a glass being half empty, whereas some people appreciate that there is half a glass of water. It totally depends on your point of view and way of thinking. People get blinded by the urge to reach success so much that they actually forget to appreciate the little things in life. If you are working and earning a handsome salary, don't just sit and complain about why you are not earning more, what you need to do to achieve that, etc. You should obviously aim high, but not at the cost of your well-being. When you practice gratitude, it increases your creativity, improves your physical health, and reduces your stress. You can start writing about the things you are grateful for in your journal every day before going to bed, make some time for appreciating your loved ones, or remind yourself of all the things you are grateful for before going to bed every day. If you are not happy with your current situation, you will not be happy in the future. You need to be happy and satisfied at first, and then only you can work on progressing further.

## 6. Always Keep Positive People Around You

When you have toxic people around you, it gets tough for you to stay in a good mood or achieve something good in life. Toxic people always find a way to pull you down and make you feel bad about yourself. You should always surround yourself with people who are encouraging and positive. When you do that, your life is going to be full of positivity.

## 7. Exercise on a Regular Basis

Start exercising regularly to maintain good health and enhancing your creativity and cognitive skills. It also increases your endurance level and boosts your energy. When you exercise regularly, your body produces more endorphins. These hormones work as anti-depressants.

## 8. Start Listening More

Effective communication is very important in maintaining both professional and personal relationships. For communicating effectively, you need to work on your listening capability first. You need to pay attention to the things said by others instead of focusing only on what you have to say. Listening to others will allow you to understand them better. When you listen to someone, it makes them understand that they are valued and that you are here to listen to them. When they feel important and valued, they also start paying attention to what you say, thereby contributing to effective communication. Don't try to show fake concentration while you are busy thinking about something else. When you listen more, you learn more.

# 9. Take a Break from Social Media (Social Media Detox)

Many studies have shown that excessive use of social media can contribute to depression. Most importantly, it wastes a lot of time because people meaninglessly scroll, swipe, and click for hours. It is a very unhealthy habit and is very bad for both physical and mental health. Sometimes you need to completely stop using social media for a while to reduce mental clutter and stress. Turn off your laptops and phones every day for a few hours. It will help you to reconnect with the surrounding world and will uplift your mood.

# 10. Start Investing More in Self-care

Make some time for yourself out of your busy schedule. It is going to boost your self-esteem, improve your mental health, and uplift your mood. You need to do at least one thing for yourself every day that will make you feel pampered and happy. You can prepare a mouth-watering meal, take a comfortable bubble bath, learn something new, or just relax while listening to music.

The moment you start introducing these habits in your daily, you will instantly see change. Remember that even a tiny step towards a positive change can give outstanding results if you stay consistent.

# Chapter 28:

# 10 Life Hacks That Will Motivate You To Do Anything

In the fast-paced race that is the world today, the most valuable asset is time, but most of our time gets wasted because of the excuses we make. Often, these excuses are legitimate, but we try to convince ourselves that these excuses are not excuses but reasons. These excuses are just a wastage of our time. Motivation is temporary. It motivates us, but with time those words no longer affect us, and we fall into the endless cycle of laziness again.

Here are a few life hacks that will motivate you to do anything.

## 1. Fixing The Sleep Cycle

Sleeping on time is one of the hardest things to do, just a few more minutes scrolling, and it's already 3 o'clock. You wouldn't want to do anything if you are tired and feel lethargic. So the first thing you need to do is to fix your sleep cycle, and even when you have fixed your sleep cycle but still feel tired, go for a 10 minutes nap. It will energize you and freshen up your brain. Now you feel ready to do anything.

## 2. Read Quotes As Often As You Can

Sometimes words are enough to motivate you through anything. Quotes often have a strong effect on us that motivates us to do anything. So print some of these and stick them on your wall or mirror and whenever you pass through the quote wall, you will feel motivated and satisfied. You can also have some of these quotes as your device's wallpaper, so now, you will get inspired whenever you use your phone.

## 3. Self-Talk Yourself To Positivity

Whenever feeling low, try to use your own words to tell yourself that you can do this. Tell yourself that you're awesome and you can do anything and have nothing to stop you. Remember your words will motivate you more than the words of others.

## 4. Set Milestones

Give yourself deadlines, set goals in parts so you don't feel burdened, and be easy on yourself. Resting is important. After crossing a milestone, give yourself appreciation and reward.

## 5. Stay Organized

Staying organized makes your mind clear and free of chaos. It allows you to focus on the work at hand. Whatever you are planning on doing, please make a list for it, and wherever you work, make that place beautiful, add a few stickers and a few new notepads. This will help you feel motivated for whatever you have to do.

## 6. Stay Active

Go for mental health walks or join a yoga club and meditate your brain; freshen it up, this will help you become more active, so the next time you want to do anything, you will take it as a challenge and feel excited about the task. As long as you feel active, things will go according to your plan.

## 7. Don't Let Your Plans Stop You From Something New

Sometimes we have a lot of plans for the future, but these plans are holding us back from something new and different. And if you are feeling stuck with your current plans, don't let these plans hold you back, change them, set new goals, and now be more practical or go for something new.

## 8. Focus On the Present

Often thinking about the future is terrifying; although it is good to have plans for the future, too much thinking can make you feel that whatever you are going for is not possible. So do what you have to do today rather than thinking of tomorrow. Focus on today and look at how far you have come, and when you have come this far, what's to stop you from going on.

## 9. Don't Let The Failures Stop You From Something New

We, human beings, feel demotivated whenever we fail or fall, and it is okay to feel that way, but you need to remember that what matters is that you don't let this failure stop you. Just accept it and move on; if you realize this isn't the thing for you, then go for something else, something new.

## 10. What If

These two small words stop us from a lot of things; when we want to try something new, the risk often stops us, our brain tells us what if we fail when facing a situation like this, remember if things could go wrong, things can also go exactly as you want. So don't let these what-ifs stop you.

What matters is how you think, and fortunately, you can change that. You can motivate yourself to do anything because you are the only one holding yourself back. Now is the time to be brave, take risks, and try new things because you can do anything.

# Chapter 29:

# Become A High Performer

We were put on this planet because we were meant to be all we could become. Human beings are the sum of their acts and achievements. But not everyone is capable of doing things to their full potential.

Every man's biggest burden is his or her unfulfilled potential.

So, what you need to become a high-performing individual in this modern era of competition is to idolize the best of the best.

You will need to understand the real-life features of a successful individual and what you need to do to become one.

If you want to be more successful in your life you need to become obsessive. Start your day with a goal and try your best to achieve it before you head to bed. You don't necessarily need to be on the right path with the first step, but you will find the best route once you have the undefeated will to find that path.

If you want to be more developed in your life you need to sleep effectively. The most successful people have a mantra of high performing routine. They don't sleep more than five hours a day and work seven days a week. They only take one day a week to sleep more just to rejuvenate their brains and body.

If you want to know if you are a high-performing successful person, look into your body language. If you find ease and leisure in everyday tasks, You are surely not standing up to your potential. If you like to sit for a conversation, start to stand. If you like to walk, start running. Get out of your comfort zone and start thinking and acting differently.

The last thing before you start your search for the right path to excellence is to set a goal every day. Increase your creativity by finding new ways to shorten the time of you becoming the better you and finally getting what you deserve.

You will eventually start seeing your life get on the track of productive learning and execution.

Change your way of treating others, especially those who are below you. If you are not a jolly person when you are broke, you can never be a jolly person when you are rich.

Never underestimate someone who is below you. You never know to whom the inspiration might take you. You have to consider the fact that life is ever-changing. Nothing ever stays the same. People never stay where they are for long.

It is the alternating nature of life that makes you keep fighting and pushing harder for better days. That is why you work hard on your skills to become a hearty human with the arms of steel.

Most people live a quiet life of desperation where they have a lot to give and a lot to say but can never get out of their cocoons.

But you are not every other person. You are the most unique soul god has created to excel at something no one has ever thought or seen before.

Start loving yourself. Stop finding faults in yourself. You are the best version of yourself, you just haven't found the right picture to look into it yet.

You want to be a high performer in every aspect of your life, here is my final advice for you.

If you push your limits in even the smallest tasks of your life, if you stretch your mind and imagination, if you can push the rules to your benefit, you might be the happiest and the most successful man humankind has ever seen.

Keep working for your dreams till the day you die. Life opens its doors to the people who knock on it. The purpose of this life is to knock on every door of opportunity and grasp that opportunity before anyone else steps forward.

You won't fulfill your desires till you make the desired effort, and that comes with a strong will and character. So, keep doing what you want to never have a regret.

# Chapter 30:

# Becoming a Leader

Wow today we're going to talk about a topic that i think might not apply to everybody, but it is one that is definitely interesting as well and good for everyone to know if they someday aspire to be a leader of sorts.

Leadership is something that does not come naturally to everyone, while some are born leaders as they say, in reality most of us requires life experiences, training, and simply good people skills in order to be an effective leader that is respected.

To be a respected leader, you have to have excellent communication skills who come across as fair and just to your employees while also being able to make tough decisions when the time comes.

I believe that leaders are not born, but their power is earned. A person who has not had the opportunities to deal with others on a social and business level can never be able to make effective decisions that serves the well-being of others. A leader in any organization is one that is able to command respect not by force but by implicit authority.

So, what are some ways that you can acquire leadership skills if you feel that you lack experience in it? Well first of all I believe that putting yourself in more social and group settings in friendly situations is a good place to start. Instead of jumping right into a work project, you can start by organizing an activity where you are in charge. For example, those that involve teamwork and team games. Maybe an escape room, or even simply taking charge by organizing a party and planning an event where you become the host, and that usually means that you are in charge of getting things in order and all the nitty gritty stuff. Planning parties, coordinating people, time management, giving instructions, preparing materials... All these little pieces require leadership to pull off. And with these practices in events that will not affect your professional career, after you get a good feel of what it is like, you can move on to taking on a leadership role in projects at school or work. And hopefully over time all these practices will add up and you will be a much more holistic leader.

Soft skills are a key part to being an effective leader as well. Apart from professional expertise at the workplace. So, I encourage you to be as proficient in your learning of people skills and mastering interpersonal communication as well as being fluent in all the intricacies and details of your job description.

If you require a higher level of leadership training, I would encourage you to sign up for a course that would put you in much more challenging situations where you will be put to the test. This may be the push that you need to get you on your path to be the leader that you always thought that you could be.

Personally, I have always been a leader, not of a team, but of my own path. That instead of following in the footsteps of someone, or taking orders from bosses, I like to take charge of what I do with my time. And how to manage my career in that fashion. As much as I would like to tell myself that i am an effective leader, more often that not, I can honestly say i wish i was better. I wish i was better at managing my time, at managing my finances, at managing my work, and I have to always upgrade my leadership skills to ensure that I am effective in what I do. That I do not waste precious time.

Your leadership goals might be different from mine. Maybe you have an aspiration to be a head of a company, or division, or to lead a group in charitable work, or to be a leader of a travel tour group. Being a leader comes in all forms and shapes, and your soft skills can definitely by transferable in all areas.

So, I challenge you to take leadership seriously and to think of ways to improve your leadership skills by placing yourself in situations where you can fine tune every aspect of your personality when dealing with others. At the end of the day, how people perceive you may be the most important factor of all.

# Chapter 31:

# Becoming High Achievers

By becoming high achievers, we become high off life, what better feeling is there than aiming for something you thought was unrealistic and then actually hitting that goal.

What better feeling is there than declaring we will do something against the perceived odds and then actually doing it.

To be a high achiever you must be a believer,

You must believe in yourself and believe that dream is possible for you.

It doesn't matter what anyone else thinks, as long as you believe,

To be a high achiever we must hunger to achieve.

To be an action taker.

Moving forward no matter what.

High achievers do not quit.

Keeping that vision in their minds eye until it becomes reality, no matter what.

Your biggest dream is protected by fear, loss and pain.

We must conquer all 3 of these impostors to walk through the door.

Not many do, most are still fighting fear and if they lose the battle, they quit.


Loss and pain are part of life.

Losses are hard on all of us.

Whether we lose possessions, whether we lose friends, whether we lose our jobs, or whether we lose family members.

Losing doesn't mean you have lost.

Losses are may be a tough pill to swallow, but they are essential because we cannot truly succeed until we fail.

We can't have the perfect relationship if we stay in a toxic one, and we can't have the life we desire until we make room by letting go of the old.


The 3 imposters that cause us so much terror are actually the first signs of our success.

So, walk through fear in courage, look at loss as an eventual gain, and know that the pain is part of the game and without it you would be weak.

Becoming a high achiever requires a single-minded focus on your goal, full commitment and an unnatural amount of persistence and work.

We must define what high achievement means to us individually, set the bar high and accept nothing less.

The achievement should not be money as money is not our currency but a tool.

The real currency is time, and your result is the time you get to experience the world's places and products, so the result should always be that.


The holiday home, the fast car, and the lifestyle of being healthy and wealthy, those are merely motivations to work towards. Like Carrots on a stick.

High achievement is individual to all of us, it means different things to each of us,

But if we are going to go for it we might as well go all out for the life we want, should we not?

I don't think we beat the odds of 1 in 400 trillion to be born, just to settle for mediocrity, did we?

Being a high achiever is in your DNA, if you can beat the odds, you can beat anything.

It is all about self-belief and confidence, we must have the confidence to take the action required and often the risk.

Risk is difficult for people and it's a difficult tight rope to walk. The line between risk and recklessness is razor thin.

Taking risks feels unnatural, not surprisingly as we all grew up in a health and safety bubble with all advice pointing towards safe and secure ways.

But the reward is often in the risk and sometimes a leap of blind faith is required. This is what stops most of us - the fear of the unknown.

The truth is the path to success is foggy and we can only ever see one step ahead, we have to imagine the result and know it's somewhere down this foggy path and keep moving forward with our new life in mind.

Know that we can make it but be aware that along the path we will be met by fear, loss and pain and the bigger our goal the bigger these monsters will be.


The top achievers financially are fanatical about their work and often work 100+ hours per week.

Some often workday and night until a project is successful.

Being a high achiever requires giving more than what is expected, standing out for the high standard of your work because being known as number 1 in your field will pay you abundantly.

Being an innovator, thinking outside the box for better practices, creating superior products to your competition because quality is more rewarding than quantity.

Maximizing the quality of your products and services to give assurance to your customers that your company is the number 1 choice.

What can we do differently to bring a better result to the table and a better experience for our customers?

We must think about questions like that because change is inevitable and without thinking like that we get left behind, but if we keep asking that, we can successfully ride the wave of change straight to the beach of our desired results.

The route to your success is by making people happy because none of us can do anything alone, we must earn the money and to earn it we must make either our employers or employees and customers happy.


To engage in self-promotion and positive interaction with those around us, we must be polite and positive with everyone, even with our competition.

Because really the only competition is ourselves and that is all we should focus on.


Self-mastery, how can I do better than yesterday?

What can I do different today that will improve my circumstances for tomorrow?

Little changes add up to a big one.

The belief and persistence towards your desired results should be 100%, I will carry on until... is the right attitude.

We must declare to ourselves that we will do this, we don't yet know how but we know that we will.

Because high achievers like yourselves know that to make it you must endure and persist until you win.

High achievers have an unnatural grit and thick skin, often doing what others won't, putting in the extra hours when others don't.

After you endure loss and conquer pain, the sky is the limit, and high achievers never settle until they are finished.